The Purpose Journal

Discover Your Destiny and Leave a Legacy

Created by
Bradley Wright PhD and Andy Best

CONTENTS

OUR STORY

Bradley is a professor of sociology. Long ago, he realized that the best way to learn something is to teach it to others. So, when he started researching purpose and meaning in life, he offered workshops to friends and family to help them discover their own purpose.

Lots of people wanted to enroll in these workshops, and in them, he heard dramatic stories of changed lives. One person quit a lucrative job to start his own business. Another came out of retirement to start a non-profit. Another rededicated herself to her family. People used what they learned to create much more purposeful lives.

Bradley was thrilled at the impact of these workshops. He wondered if there were other ways of helping people find more purpose in their lives. The idea of a daily guided journal came to mind. The process of finding purpose is often described as a journey, and the everyday nature of a journal fits this well. Ideally, this journal would both guide people in reflecting on their lives as well as give them lessons about purpose.

He quickly realized that this wasn't something he could do by himself and remembered Andy, a favorite student from years before. On a whim, Bradley reached out to Andy. Andy, coincidentally, had started listening to Bradley's podcast, The School of Purpose.

Andy recently became a father. As with many people, parenthood has moved him to engage in what matters most in life. He understood his purpose as a husband and father, but was there more? He wanted a greater picture of what purpose truly meant in his life.

Andy felt that he was on a journey with an unknown destination ahead of him and appreciated the idea of having a journal to guide him along the way.

So, they got to work. What they thought would be a six-month project ended up being two years as they dove deep into the process of finding life purpose. Numerous beta testers also contributed to the creation of this journal, the result of which is what you're holding now.

THIS JOURNAL AS YOUR GUIDE

This journal is your guide for discovering and enacting purpose in life.

Every day, it gives you practical steps for understanding what matters most to you and what you should do about it. These steps are drawn from social research as well as best practices in finding purpose.

This practical approach demystifies the purpose-seeking process. It enables you to translate your desire for more purpose into intentional movement forward.

The journal also gives lessons about the basics of finding purpose—what purpose is, what it feels like, and why it's so important.

As you write every day, you'll examine your life in new ways. You'll see things that you never have before. These will be clues that point you in the way that is most purposeful for you.

You'll practice viewing each day through the lens of purpose. In the morning, you'll plan for what will make a more purposeful day. In the evening, you'll look back on the day and evaluate what was and wasn't purposeful.

Purpose is not one-size-fits-all. It's unique for every person. This is why you need to daily reflect on your life and what matters most.

As you understand more of what matters to you, you'll make plans for implementing it into your life. Ultimately, purpose is enacted, not just understood. The journal gives you prompts for projecting how you will take action on what you're learning.

As practical as we want to be in finding purpose, there's still a mysterious element to it. Sometimes things happen that we can't predict. This journal guides you in your search for purpose, and when you search for purpose, it somehow finds you.

HERE'S WHAT TO EXPECT

This journal covers twenty-one weeks, and each week has a similar rhythm. Here's what will happen:

THE START OF THE WEEK

Introduction
Each week starts with a brief introduction about the topic covered that week. It gives you basic information about it and orients you to what you'll be doing that week.

A Story
Then, you'll read an inspirational story about someone who has lived with significant purpose within the theme for that week. This is to give you a sense of what is possible with purpose in your own life.

THE FIRST SIX DAYS

For the first six days of each week, you will answer four questions.

Question 1: The Learning Question. This question changes every day, reflecting the topic of that week. It examines purpose from different perspectives, and it uses your life as a laboratory to teach you how to find and enact purpose.

Question 2: The Planning Question. This question has you explore how you can take smalls step to more fully realize your purpose. Purpose doesn't occur in one big moment but, instead, in small increments that get us closer and closer to our realization. By planning small things we can do each day, we can ensure we are intentional about the path we're taking.

Question 3: The Rating Question. This question has you rate your experience of purpose that day. A rating of -2 means "not at all," -1 is "a little," 0 is "some," +1 is "a good amount," and +2 is "a lot." By rating your days, you'll see patterns of when you experience purpose and what affects your purpose levels. This, in turn, gives you insight as to what you can do to increase your daily experience of purpose.

Question 4: The Recognition Question. This question asks you to look back on your day and identify something that you did that really mattered and explain why it mattered. Answering this question trains you to recognize what matters most to you. This pattern recognition gives you a deeper understanding of purpose.

THE SEVENTH DAY

Reflections

The seventh day of each week prompts you to reflect on the previous week.

You'll be asked questions about what you've learned about yourself and your purpose that week. This is a chance to reflect on the broader themes of purpose in your life.

OCCASIONAL OVERVIEWS

At several points, you will be asked to step back and examine the broader themes of purpose in your life. In doing this, you'll integrate what you've learned in the previous weeks. These overviews happen at the end of weeks four, ten, and twenty-one.

HOW TO USE THIS JOURNAL

WHEN TO DO IT

The most effective way to fill out this journal is to do it twice a day. You do the first two questions in the morning—before your day gets going and you can plan for it. Then, you do the second two questions in the evening—when your day is over and you can reflect on it.

Some people, however, use the journal just once a day. It could be in the morning when you reflect on the previous day and plan for the coming day. It could also be in the evening when you reflect on the current day and plan for the next one.

MAKE THIS JOURNAL A HABIT

Fit the journal into your existing routine.
Pick a time linked to something that you're already doing. For example, in the morning, do the journal after you brush your teeth or while having your breakfast. Or, at night, do it when you get home from work or when you get ready for bed. This makes the journal part of your daily routine.

Keep the journal in a visible place.
Life is busy. It's easy to overlook things. Keep the journal in a place where you'll regularly see it, such as on a nightstand or table. Seeing the journal regularly will remind you to do it.

Spend five minutes a day.
The questions in this journal are thought-provoking. You might want to put a lot of time into them. This is fine, but don't overdo it. You don't want to feel obliged to put a lot of time into it each day. This will make it feel like a burden. Aim for doing five minutes a day. Be consistent. The payoff comes over time.

Reward yourself.
Celebrate doing the journal each day. Appreciate your effort. Value what you're learning. A simple reward that you can give yourself each day is to draw a happy face at the bottom of your page when you finish your entries. This small reward will help bring you back the next day.

SHARE YOUR JOURNEY – STEP 1

DO THE JOURNAL WITH OTHER PEOPLE

As you're thinking about how you want to do this journal, you might assume that you have to do it by yourself. After all, it's about you and your purpose in life.

Consider doing it with someone else.

When we share our purpose journal with others, it actually helps us. People who know us and love us remind us of who we really are. They have insights into how we can live more fully. They encourage us when we're tired and discouraged.

Sharing our journey with others also helps them. When people see us pursuing what matters most in our life, it inspires them to do the same thing. What they see happening in us becomes a possibility for them.

Sharing our journey also strengthens our relationships with people. It moves us beyond shallow daily interactions, and we get to know them at a deeper level. We move forward together, focused on our deepest values.

You could:

» Invite someone to do the journal at the same time you are. Then, you can meet regularly to share what you're learning.

» Have a recurring journal meet-up where you review your reflection questions with a group and discuss how you'll take steps to pursue more purpose in your lives.

» Think of a creative way to share your journey with those closest to you!

Doing this journal with others will increase your self-understanding as well as connect you more deeply with others.

Later, we'll suggest two other ways to share your purpose journey with other people.

WHAT IS PURPOSE?

What, exactly, is purpose in life?

The concept of purpose is defined in different ways by different people, though typically, definitions have the following three components:

1. *Personally Meaningful.* Purpose in life is significant. It matters to us. It is more important than other things in life. This is a feeling rather than a mental calculation. In fact, what feels most important to us can be at odds with what we "think" we should do. The experience of purpose is highly individual. An activity that is profoundly meaningful for one person might be drudgery for someone else. This is why we each have to discover purpose for ourselves. It's personally meaningful, not one-size-fits-all.

2. *Goals & Plans.* Once we know what matters most to us, what do we do with it? The answer is simple: *something.* Discovering our life's purpose starts with knowing what is most meaningful and significant to us, but then we have to do something about it. We use it to guide our actions. We make plans and set goals based on what matters most to us. Life purpose is our ultimate aim in life. We work toward bringing it about more fully in our lives. If we know what matters but don't act upon it, we don't have purpose. We're just dreaming. Life purpose points us forward.

3. *Beyond Yourself.* Life purpose is profoundly personal and introspective, but it isn't just about us. It means going beyond ourselves. This can mean transforming who we are. It can also mean making life better for other people. It's making a difference, it's making a contribution, and this contribution can take many forms. It can be directly helping other people, creating beauty, tending to the physical world—whatever is most meaningful for us. Purpose has us acting beyond our own selfish interests to make the world a better place in some way.

The metaphors commonly used for purpose convey what it is... a journey forward down a path created for us. It's an internal compass that points to what matters most.

MULTIPLE PURPOSES

A common misconception is that we have one single purpose in life, and once we find it—and only when we find it will we be fulfilled.

This belief is inaccurate and unhelpful for a variety of reasons. Believing it results in a lot of stress. We compare different opportunities and wonder to ourselves whether any one of them is "the one" for us.

Also, it puts a lot of pressure on what we're doing. There's no single role or activity that will meet all of our needs for purpose and meaning in our lives. This belief leads to continual dissatisfaction.

In reality, we have many opportunities for purpose in our lives. In fact, we have more opportunities than we can realize! Indeed, as we explore what is purposeful in our lives, we soon find that we have more possible sources of purpose than we could possibly pursue in one lifetime.

We have different purposes across different domains of our lives. It's unlikely that a single activity will give us deep purpose for our career, relationships, spirituality, and self-development. Instead, we might need to pursue the purpose of each one separately.

Even if we do find a single source of purpose in some area of our life, it's unlikely that it will stay unchanged forever. Careers change, relationships change, and even *we* change.

In the end, we would do well to think of finding multiple purposes for our life rather than finding one single purpose. This opens us up to a wide range of possibilities.

This journal uses the language "purpose in life" out of the conventional. Nonetheless, it aims to guide you in identifying the constellation of activities and relationships in your life that might give you a deep sense of purpose.

PURPOSE WILL CHANGE YOUR LIFE

There are good reasons to put time and effort into finding more life purpose.

Purpose makes our lives fuller. It gives us the "why" of existence. It is what matters most. When we have it, we feel contentment and energy. Life doesn't just pass by unimportantly. It is lived as it is meant to be lived.

Purpose makes the world more whole. It results in beauty and knowledge. It moves people and mountains. It connects people. It makes other people's lives better. It leaves a legacy.

Research has found that great things happen when people find purpose in their lives.

People with more purpose are happier, more satisfied, fulfilled, grateful, and resilient. They are less stressed, anxious, depressed, and bored.

People with purpose have stronger immune systems, lower cholesterol levels, and better sleep.

People with purpose are more altruistic, involved in society, successful in school, and better at work.

People with purpose even live longer!

Think of having purpose as a superpower for living a richer, more meaningful life!

FINDING YOUR PURPOSE(S)

Do you want to find more purpose in your life?

Looking for purpose is beautiful. It's full of promise and hope. It is exhilarating. We want a better life, and we want meaning. We feel as if we're here on earth for a reason, and we want to live it out. What matters more in life than finding what matters most?

Looking for purpose is also terrifying. When we start doing it, we feel like our lives are coming apart. We feel confused and upset. The quest for purpose can change every aspect of our lives, and this produces uncertainty and self-doubt. In this sense, living *without* purpose is easier than living *with* purpose. When we look for purpose, we start off not knowing where to go or how to get there. We wonder if we even have a purpose. It's all too much!

While finding purpose isn't easy, it is possible. With practice, we learn to recognize what matters most in our lives, and we explore how to have more of it. Though the future is murky, we press on—having faith that we will find the right destination if we keep at it. We push on when we encounter resistance. We reinterpret the difficulties that we face. Rather than signs that we should stop what we're doing, these difficulties are opportunities to grow stronger. The process of finding purpose causes us to question everything in our lives. This is challenging. However, if we continue to move forward, we incorporate more and more purpose into our lives until, at some point, we realize that we're truly living with purpose.

WHERE ARE YOU NOW?

Everybody starts their purpose journey somewhere. You have some understanding of what matters most to you, and you want more. Writing out how you understand your life purpose now serves you well moving forward. It is something that you can build upon. Don't worry about how specific or vague it is. Whatever you write will be helpful.

What do I understand my life purpose to be now?

_____

_____

_____

_____

_____

_____

_____

_____

_____

_____

_____

_____

_____

_____

_____

_____

_____

_____

_____

_____

_____

WHY DO YOU WANT PURPOSE?

As you prepare to journey into greater purpose, it's a good time to reflect on why you want more life purpose. Being clear on this helps motivate you to do the hard work of finding purpose. It will also give you satisfaction as you discover the important parts of your life.

Why do I want more purpose in my life?

Week #1

RECOGNIZING PURPOSE IN YOUR LIFE

Each week has its own theme. The theme of the first week is: "Recognizing Purpose in Your Life."

As you've learned, purpose is a combination of what is meaningful to us, our plans and goals for the future, and ways we can contribute to the lives of other people and the world.

As such, purpose has various characteristics, and knowing these characteristics makes it identify in our lives.

Purpose matters. It feels significant. It's found among the things in life that are most important to us.

Purpose is directive. It's a guide to the way forward. It gives direction and goals. It's an inner GPS.

Purpose is impactful. It changes lives. It makes the world a better place.

Purpose is authentic. It's who a person really is. It's values, passions, and interests.

Purpose is multidimensional. It's found in multiple areas of life, including work, relationships, spirituality, and self.

Purpose is social. It connects us. It brings us together for a larger cause.

This week, you'll analyze which aspects of your life fit with purpose.

Each week starts with a story that illustrates the theme for that week. This week's story demonstrates the essential nature of purpose and its power to transform lives.

FINDING PURPOSE IN PRISON

Quan Huynh was convicted of murder. He killed a man as a gang member and was serving a life sentence in the California prison system.

Quan spent his first eleven years in prison doing what he had been doing before—acting violently and intimidating others. He didn't want anyone to bother him.

One day, he learned that his beloved grandfather had passed away and, a short while later, his brother had a daughter. This poignant combination of life and death stirred Quan to start asking deeper questions about how he was living his life.

Something shifted inside. He knew that he would never get out of prison. It was a mandatory life sentence. Still, he wanted to live a better life. He wanted his life to mean something. He yearned for beauty and significance. He knew that his life was meant for more than he was living. He wanted purpose.

Quan changed his life. He decided to do what mattered most every day—even though he was still behind razor wire. So, he decided to make some changes. When he talked to other people, he chose to listen more than he spoke. When he did speak, he only spoke the truth—no more deceit. He started spiritual practices such as meditation. He read books about the saints and other people who had lived profound lives. He helped other incarcerated men when he could.

His body was in prison, but Quan wanted his soul to be free.

Years later, his fortune improved. The State of California changed its laws so that men like Quan could apply for parole. The parole hearing was tense. Quan didn't think that he would get out. Eventually, though, the parole board realized that Quan was a different man. Quan was released after serving 16 years for his murder conviction.

Quan frequently returns to prison. He helps the incarcerated in their own quest for a better life. He's even written a book, *Sparrow in the Razor Wire: Finding Freedom from Within While Serving a Life Sentence*, to share the lessons that he's learned. He demonstrates what can happen when a life is devoted to what truly matters.

"

This above all: to thine own self be true. William Shakespeare

"

Which of my routine activities feel most meaningful to me?

_____

_____

_____

_____

What small thing can I do today to live more purposefully?

_____

_____

_____

_____

Did I experience purpose in the past day? (Circle one)

-2   -1   0   +1   +2

What's one thing I did that mattered to me? Why did it matter?

_____

_____

_____

_____

"

Meaningfulness arises from a sense that events are particularly profound, significant, or promote a feeling of transcendence. Laura King

"

What do I do in life that feels most authentic to who I am?

_____

_____

_____

_____

What small thing can I do this day to live more purposefully?

_____

_____

_____

_____

Did I experience purpose in the past day? (Circle one)

-2   -1   0   +1   +2

What's one thing I did that mattered to me? Why did it matter?

_____

_____

_____

_____

"

A person without purpose is like a ship without a rudder. Thomas Carlyle

"

How does my sense of purpose impact my plans for the future?

_____

_____

_____

_____

What small thing can I do today to live more purposefully?

_____

_____

_____

_____

Did I experience purpose in the past day? (Circle one)

-2   -1   0   +1   +2

What's one thing I did that mattered to me? Why did it matter?

_____

_____

_____

_____

"

The notion that we have only one thing we are meant for limits us from fulfilling our greatness. Shannon Kaiser

"

In which areas of my life would I most like to have more purpose?

_____

_____

_____

_____

What small thing can I do this day to live more purposefully?

_____

_____

_____

_____

Did I experience purpose in the past day? (Circle one)

-2   -1   0   +1   +2

What's one thing I did that mattered to me? Why did it matter?

_____

_____

_____

_____

"

*We have been created for a purpose; for great things:
to love and be loved.* Mother Teresa

"

How can living purposefully connect me with others?

_____
_____
_____
_____

What small thing can I do today to live more purposefully?

_____
_____
_____
_____

Did I experience purpose in the past day? (Circle one)

-2   -1   0   +1   +2

What's one thing I did that mattered to me? Why did it matter?

_____
_____
_____
_____

"

Service is the rent we pay for being. It is the very purpose of life, and not something you do in your spare time. Marian Wright Edelman

"

How can living purposefully benefit other people?

_____

_____

_____

_____

What small thing can I do this day to live more purposefully?

_____

_____

_____

_____

Did I experience purpose in the past day? (Circle one)

-2   -1   0   +1   +2

What's one thing I did that mattered to me? Why did it matter?

_____

_____

_____

_____

WEEK 1 REFLECTION

If someone asked me to explain to them the concept of purpose,
what would I say?

_____

_____

_____

_____

_____

_____

Looking over what I wrote this week, what can I learn about purpose in my life?

_____

_____

_____

_____

_____

Based on what I've learned this week, what would it look like for me to
live with more purpose?

_____

_____

_____

_____

_____

_____

Week #2

CORE VALUES

Values are the heart of purpose.

When something is valued, it is important. It matters to us. It is worth more than other things.

People have many different types of values. We can value integrity, courage, loyalty, compassion, spirituality, generosity, and plenty of other desirable personal characteristics.

How do we identify our values? This can be surprisingly difficult because there are so many possible values that we can hold. We start by carefully examining ourselves and our lives.

When we live purposefully, we put into action the things that we most value. We match our actions to what matters most to us.

When we don't do this, something inside of us starts to wither. We feel anxious, disheartened, and angst-ridden.

Any given value can be lived out in multiple ways. Two people holding the same values can live very different lives. Not only that, but we can change how we express our values over time.

Knowing what we value and living it out both make for a great life and are the work of a lifetime.

This week, you will explore your underlying values and how they connect to your purpose.

Audrey's story illustrates how the same values can be expressed differently.

UNDERLYING VALUES ACROSS CAREERS

Audrey Seymour enjoys her work, and she's really good at it. She's a life coach at the True Purpose Institute who specializes in helping people discover their purpose in life.

When working with clients, Audrey starts off by having them identify what they fear in pursuing purpose. Living purposefully requires change, so inevitably, fears arise. Audrey shows them how to address their fears.

Then, Audrey has clients get in touch with an inner source of wisdom. This source of wisdom varies by person. It could be intuition, the soul, God, or something else, depending on the client's worldview. This inner wisdom is a guide to greater purpose.

As her clients understand what is purposeful for them, Audrey has them create a plan for living it out. This plan involves goals and strategies and moves people into living out what matters most to them.

Audrey hasn't always been a purpose coach. She started her career as a software project manager. As a project manager, she developed a reputation for being good at working with dysfunctional teams. When a team experienced conflict, company leadership sent in Audrey. She engaged each team member separately. Then, she coaxed, inspired, and guided the team to move forward together.

At first glance, being a team manager and a purpose coach seem like very different jobs. For Audrey, however, they are rooted in the same values. Both involve working with disparate units that are not functioning together well and then helping them resolve their differences. Just as people on a team need to work together, so too do the different aspects of a person's personality. When the parts of a personality are at odds with each other, it's difficult to move forward in life. As a coach, Audrey helps people to bring their personalities and dreams into coherent, productive wholes.

"

*I have learned that as long as I hold fast to my beliefs and values
– and follow my own moral compass – then the only expectations
I need to live up to are my own.* Michelle Obama

"

Which values are most important to me?

_____

_____

_____

_____

What small thing can I do today to live more purposefully?

_____

_____

_____

_____

Did I experience purpose in the past day? (Circle one)

-2   -1   0   +1   +2

What's one thing I did that mattered to me? Why did it matter?

_____

_____

_____

_____

"

The most important ingredient we put into any relationship is not what we say or what we do, but what we are. Stephen Covey

"

What do I value most for my relationships?

_____
_____
_____
_____

What small thing can I do this day to live more purposefully?

_____
_____
_____
_____

Did I experience purpose in the past day? (Circle one)

-2   -1   0   +1   +2

What's one thing I did that mattered to me? Why did it matter?

_____
_____
_____
_____

"

*If, in fact, the work you love is calling, the question then becomes:
are you listening?* Laurence G. Boldt

"

What do I value most for my work?

_____

_____

_____

_____

What small thing can I do today to live more purposefully?

_____

_____

_____

_____

Did I experience purpose in the past day? (Circle one)

-2   -1   0   +1   +2

What's one thing I did that mattered to me? Why did it matter?

_____

_____

_____

_____

"

"He faced each day's issues in light of eternal and universal values."
Louis Fischer on Gandhi.

"

Which values would I like to pass along to other people?

_____

_____

_____

_____

What small thing can I do this day to live more purposefully?

_____

_____

_____

_____

Did I experience purpose in the past day? (Circle one)

-2   -1   0   +1   +2

What's one thing I did that mattered to me? Why did it matter?

_____

_____

_____

_____

"

Don't tell me where your priorities are. Show me where you spend your money and I'll tell you what they are. James W. Frick

"

What do my spending habits tell me about my values?

_____
_____
_____
_____

What small thing can I do today to live more purposefully?

_____
_____
_____
_____

Did I experience purpose in the past day? (Circle one)

-2   -1   0   +1   +2

What's one thing I did that mattered to me? Why did it matter?

_____
_____
_____
_____

"

*The most important choices you'll ever make are how
you use your time.* David Kekich

"

What does my use of time tell me about my values?

_____

_____

_____

_____

What small thing can I do this day to live more purposefully?

_____

_____

_____

_____

Did I experience purpose in the past day? (Circle one)

-2   -1   0   +1   +2

What's one thing I did that mattered to me? Why did it matter?

_____

_____

_____

_____

WEEK 2 REFLECTION

How much am I living out my core values in life?

_____

_____

_____

_____

_____

_____

Looking over what I wrote this week, what can I learn about purpose in my life?

_____

_____

_____

_____

_____

Based on what I've learned this week, what would it look like for me to
live with more purpose?

_____

_____

_____

_____

_____

_____

_____

Week #3

EXPERIENCING PURPOSE

Experiencing purpose is distinctive. It feels different than other things that happen in our lives.

It's important to know what purpose feels like because recognizing what we already have makes it easier to find more of it.

It's as if experiencing purpose has symptoms. Things are felt that aren't otherwise felt. It's like having a cold. You know you're sick when you have symptoms: a runny nose, sore throat, and nasal congestion.

Likewise, having purpose gives its own far more pleasant symptoms that we can use to identify it.

Some of the feelings (or "symptoms") people commonly report experiencing when they are acting purposefully are:

» Increased emotional energy

» Greater engagement in an activity

» A feeling of passion

» A sense of authenticity

» Doing something that just "feels right"

This week, you will examine how you experience feelings of purpose.

Nick's story illustrates feelings associated with purpose.

PURPOSE ENERGIZING A CAREER

Nick Copenhaver had a plan for his career that was both ambitious and artificial. He planned to become a corporate lawyer. He wasn't particularly interested in law or even the corporate world. Rather, he just wanted to make a lot of money. He figured that he wouldn't like any job that he did anyway—it was work, after all—so why not do something that at least paid well?

This made sense to his head, but it didn't stir his heart. Sometimes Nick wondered if there was something out there that was better.

On a whim, he signed up to do research with his professor. Nick studied how purpose is defined, how people experience it, and what can be done to have more of it. Along the way, Nick started applying what he was learning to his own life.

After months of thinking about purpose, Nick realized one day that he wanted to change careers. Growing up, Nick was a star baseball player. While he didn't want to be in competitive sports, he was still interested in health and the body. He wanted to help other people become healthier. He wanted to become a dietician.

Nick was very happy to plan a career that meant something to him, but this change created problems. He was entering his senior year, and there wasn't much time left to change what he studied. So, he had to work hard. He took extra classes. He finished off his original economics major, and he also took science courses to prepare for graduate school in nutrition.

As he worked, Nick noticed a difference. When he was preparing to become a lawyer—a career that didn't engage him—studying was a grind. He struggled to make himself do it.

Now that he was doing something that mattered to him, Nick was eager to work hard. He did the assigned work and extra work on top of that because he found it so engaging.

Nick was experiencing purpose.

"

Why did you get out of bed this morning? Simon Sinek

"

Which activities most energize me when I do them?

_____

_____

_____

_____

What small thing can I do today to live more purposefully?

_____

_____

_____

_____

Did I experience purpose in the past day? (Circle one)

-2   -1   0   +1   +2

What's one thing I did that mattered to me? Why did it matter?

_____

_____

_____

_____

> *Flow is being completely involved in an activity for its own sake. The ego falls away. Time flies. Every action, movement, and thought follows inevitably from the previous one.* Mihaly Csikszentmihalyi

Which activities fully engage me when I do them?

What small thing can I do this day to live more purposefully?

Did I experience purpose in the past day? (Circle one)

-2   -1   0   +1   +2

What's one thing I did that mattered to me? Why did it matter?

"

You already found your passion, you're just ignoring it. Mark Manson

"

When do I feel most passionate about what I'm doing?

_____

_____

_____

_____

What small thing can I do today to live more purposefully?

_____

_____

_____

_____

Did I experience purpose in the past day? (Circle one)

-2   -1   0   +1   +2

What's one thing I did that mattered to me? Why did it matter?

_____

_____

_____

_____

"
Everything in your life informs you what your purpose is. How do you know it's your purpose? It feels like it's the right space for you. It feels like 'This is what I should be doing; this is where I feel most myself.' Oprah Winfrey
"

What do I do that feels most authentic to who I am?

_____

_____

_____

_____

What small thing can I do this day to live more purposefully?

_____

_____

_____

_____

Did I experience purpose in the past day? (Circle one)

-2   -1   0   +1   +2

What's one thing I did that mattered to me? Why did it matter?

_____

_____

_____

_____

"
Don't ask yourself what the world needs; ask yourself what makes you come alive. And then go and do that. Because what the world needs is people who have come alive. Howard Thurman
"

What does it feel like when I'm doing something purposeful?

_____
_____
_____
_____

What small thing can I do today to live more purposefully?

_____
_____
_____
_____

Did I experience purpose in the past day? (Circle one)

-2   -1   0   +1   +2

What's one thing I did that mattered to me? Why did it matter?

_____
_____
_____
_____

"

*The greatest tragedy in life is not death, but a life
without a purpose.* Myles Munroe

"

What does it feel like when I'm doing something that isn't purposeful?

_____
_____
_____
_____

What small thing can I do this day to live more purposefully?

_____
_____
_____
_____

Did I experience purpose in the past day? (Circle one)

-2   -1   0   +1   +2

What's one thing I did that mattered to me? Why did it matter?

_____
_____
_____
_____

WEEK 3 REFLECTION

How can I use my awareness of experiencing purpose to find more of it in my life?

Looking over what I wrote this week, what can I learn about purpose in my life?

Based on what I've learned this week, what would it look like for me to live with more purpose?

FINDING PURPOSE THROUGHOUT OUR LIVES

We don't experience just one purpose in just one area of life. That's one of the things that makes purpose so amazing. We can experience it everywhere—in our careers, relationships, service, hobbies, spirituality, finances, and so on.

When people ask, "What should I do with my life," they often limit their inquiry to their career. Yes, we want purpose in our careers, but it's so much more than that!

While we want to have deep purpose throughout our lives, most people vary in their experience of purpose. They'll have more in some areas than others.

Exploring how we are already experiencing purpose across our life lets us know where we are starting. Some areas might be doing pretty well already. Other areas may need more work.

This week, you will examine what you find purposeful in different areas of your life.

Bob's story demonstrates how purpose can transform an area of life.

THE LIFE-CHANGING POWER OF KNOWING YOUR PURPOSE

Bob Turner was 24 years old and working on Wall Street. When walking through a cemetery, a gravestone's message impacted him deeply: "As You Stand There Now, So Once Did I." Soon after that, he had a mentor who had him do an exercise to explore what he wanted most in life. In the exercise, Bob wrote his obituary.

Bob wasn't dying, but this exercise gave him a different perspective on his life. By anticipating how he'd look back on his life, he could focus on what was truly important.

After he wrote his obituary, Bob realized that he didn't really want to spend his career on Wall Street. He wanted to help other people more directly. In particular, he wanted to teach people to help still other people. This meant leadership training. Bob knew that if he could effectively mentor leaders, his impact on the world would spread like ripples in a pond.

He thought about this for several years. Then, at age 33, he decided to give his life to training leaders. He quit his job on Wall Street and joined The Navigators, a Christian organization, as a staff person.

Bob spent the next 40 years mentoring leaders worldwide.

Bob spent twelve years in South Africa at the end of the Apartheid Era, where he worked in the township of Soweto. These were difficult times for the people there. Bob built relationships with young people and trained them to be leaders. He did this so effectively that the people he mentored have become prominent leaders in business, government, and church. Not long ago, a large church outside of Johannesburg hosted a thirty-year celebration of Bob's impact on so many people's lives.

Today, Bob is back home in Massachusetts. Rather than retiring, he continues to work for The Navigators. He regularly meets with ministers and other leaders to mentor them. His influence continues to spread.

"

*It's not enough to have lived. We should be determined
to live for something.* Winston S. Churchill

"

In which areas of life do I have the most purpose? In which do I have the least?

_____

_____

_____

_____

What small thing can I do today to live more purposefully?

_____

_____

_____

_____

Did I experience purpose in the past day? (Circle one)

-2   -1   0   +1   +2

What's one thing I did that mattered to me? Why did it matter?

_____

_____

_____

_____

"

Everyone has been made for some particular work, and the desire for that work has been put in every heart. Jalaluddin Rumi

"

What do I find purposeful in my work (or other full-time activity)?

_____

_____

_____

_____

What small thing can I do this day to live more purposefully?

_____

_____

_____

_____

Did I experience purpose in the past day? (Circle one)

-2   -1   0   +1   +2

What's one thing I did that mattered to me? Why did it matter?

_____

_____

_____

_____

"

The purpose of life is to contribute in some way to making things better. Robert F. Kennedy

"

What am I already doing to make the world a better place?

_____
_____
_____
_____

What small thing can I do today to live more purposefully?

_____
_____
_____
_____

Did I experience purpose in the past day? (Circle one)

-2   -1   0   +1   +2

What's one thing I did that mattered to me? Why did it matter?

_____
_____
_____
_____

"

It's your unlimited power to care and to love that can make the biggest difference in the quality of your life. Tony Robbins

"

What do I find purposeful in my relationships with other people?

_____

_____

_____

_____

What small thing can I do this day to live more purposefully?

_____

_____

_____

_____

Did I experience purpose in the past day? (Circle one)

-2   -1   0   +1   +2

What's one thing I did that mattered to me? Why did it matter?

_____

_____

_____

_____

"

Do not wish to be anything but what you are, and try to be that perfectly. St. Francis of De Sales

"

What do I find purposeful in my own personal development?

_____
_____
_____
_____

What small thing can I do today to live more purposefully?

_____
_____
_____
_____

Did I experience purpose in the past day? (Circle one)

-2   -1   0   +1   +2

What's one thing I did that mattered to me? Why did it matter?

_____
_____
_____
_____

"

The soul which has no fixed purpose in life is lost; to be everywhere, is to be nowhere. Michel de Montaigne

"

What do I find purposeful in my spiritual life?

_____

_____

_____

_____

What small thing can I do this day to live more purposefully?

_____

_____

_____

_____

Did I experience purpose in the past day? (Circle one)

-2   -1   0   +1   +2

What's one thing I did that mattered to me? Why did it matter?

_____

_____

_____

_____

WEEK 4 REFLECTION

How does my sense of purpose vary across areas of my life?

_____

_____

_____

_____

_____

_____

Looking over what I wrote this week, what can I learn about purpose in my life?

_____

_____

_____

_____

_____

Based on what I've learned this week, what would it look like for me to live with more purpose?

_____

_____

_____

_____

_____

_____

ONE-MONTH REFLECTION

Congratulations! You've done this journal for four weeks! The time and effort that you have put into it will move you forward into what matters most in your life.

At this time, step back and reflect on what you've learned so far. Review what you've written, and look for patterns and insights.

What have I learned about my life purpose?

_____

_____

_____

_____

_____

_____

_____

_____

_____

_____

_____

_____

_____

_____

_____

_____

_____

_____

_____

_____

_____

_____

As a result, how do I want to live my life differently?

_____
_____
_____
_____
_____
_____
_____
_____
_____
_____
_____
_____
_____
_____
_____
_____
_____
_____
_____
_____
_____
_____
_____
_____

REMEMBERING CHILDHOOD

Children have beautiful dreams for their lives, but what happens to these dreams when they grow up?

It's all too easy to dismiss our childhood passions as passing fancies. We think that we have outgrown them.

In reality, childhood dreams are seeds of interest that can extend into adulthood.

Of course, how we want to express these interests can change with age. A child who wants to be a firefighter might grow into an adult who finds another career that helps other people.

Remembering our childhood passions gives us insight into our current passions. It's a way of finding things that still matter but that we have put aside.

Who knows? It might be time to pick up these interests again.

This week, you will explore the purposeful interests of your childhood.

*Julie's story illustrates how reengaging childhood
interests can lead to a more purposeful life.*

REDISCOVERING A CHILDHOOD LOVE OF READING

Julie Cyzewski grew up loving to read. She especially loved fiction. Books took her to new places. They gave her a different perspective on the world. She felt deeply passionate about them.

Her love of books continued with her education. English classes were always her favorite in high school, and she majored in English literature in college.

After she graduated, Julie looked for a job that would allow her to help other people. She's a moral person, and she decided that the best choice would be teaching students who struggled to succeed in school. It would connect her with needy people in society. So, she worked as a special education teacher at an elementary school.

Something wasn't right, however. While she cared deeply about helping other people, working in this context never really felt right. She was neither happy with it nor fulfilled by it.

Outside of work, Julie read constantly—especially fiction. She even read books on literature theory. She had chosen to move away from literature, but somehow it wouldn't go away.

Finally, Julie returned to her childhood passion. She quit her job and returned to school to get a Ph.D. in English literature. This wasn't easy. Her family had to relocate three times. Nonetheless, she finished her Ph.D. in a top literature program, and she got a job as a tenure-track professor where she is now.

Julie still wants to help people, but now she does it in a way that fits her childhood dreams. She teaches her students new ideas that enable them to think differently about themselves and their world. This is deeply meaningful to her.

"

I sometimes think that childhood is where the real meaning of life is located, and that we, adults, are its servants - that's our purpose. Karl Ove Knausgard

"

What are some of the things that I loved doing as a child?

_____
_____
_____
_____

What small thing can I do today to live more purposefully?

_____
_____
_____
_____

Did I experience purpose in the past day? (Circle one)

-2   -1   0   +1   +2

What's one thing I did that mattered to me? Why did it matter?

_____
_____
_____
_____

"

*Dare to err and to dream. Deep meaning often lies
in childish plays.* Friedrich Schiller

"

What did I feel deeply and passionately about as a child?

_____

_____

_____

_____

What small thing can I do this day to live more purposefully?

_____

_____

_____

_____

Did I experience purpose in the past day? (Circle one)

-2   -1   0   +1   +2

What's one thing I did that mattered to me? Why did it matter?

_____

_____

_____

_____

"

Everyone who gives up a serious childhood dream ... lives the rest of their life with a sense of loss, with nagging what ifs. Glenn Kurtz

"

When I was a child, what did I want to do when I grew up?

_____

_____

_____

_____

What small thing can I do today to live more purposefully?

_____

_____

_____

_____

Did I experience purpose in the past day? (Circle one)

-2   -1   0   +1   +2

What's one thing I did that mattered to me? Why did it matter?

_____

_____

_____

_____

"

It is your birthright to have a life of meaning and purpose. David Simon

"

Which of my childhood interests still intrigue me?

_____

_____

_____

What small thing can I do this day to live more purposefully?

_____

_____

_____

Did I experience purpose in the past day? (Circle one)

-2   -1   0   +1   +2

What's one thing I did that mattered to me? Why did it matter?

_____

_____

_____

_____

> *When you have a childhood dream that still burns and tugs at your heart when you're an adult, you owe it to yourself to pursue and achieve this dream.* Robert Cheeke

What are aspects of my life now that would have made me sad as a child?

_____
_____
_____
_____

What small thing can I do today to live more purposefully?

_____
_____
_____
_____

Did I experience purpose in the past day? (Circle one)

-2   -1   0   +1   +2

What's one thing I did that mattered to me? Why did it matter?

_____
_____
_____
_____

"

Never lose the child-like wonder. It's just too important.
It's what drives us. Help others. Randy Pausch

"

What are aspects of my life now that would have made me happy as a child?

_____
_____
_____
_____

What small thing can I do this day to live more purposefully?

_____
_____
_____
_____

Did I experience purpose in the past day? (Circle one)

-2   -1   0   +1   +2

What's one thing I did that mattered to me? Why did it matter?

_____
_____
_____
_____

WEEK 5 REFLECTION

How can I use my childhood dreams to guide my future purpose?

_____

_____

_____

_____

_____

_____

Looking over what I wrote this week, what can I learn about purpose in my life?

_____

_____

_____

_____

_____

Based on what I've learned this week, what would it look like for me to
live with more purpose?

_____

_____

_____

_____

_____

_____

_____

Week #6

LEARNING FROM THE PAST

Our past feeds our current sense of purpose, like roots to a plant.

What we've experienced so far in life—events, successes, failures, joys, trials, and everything else—makes us into who we are and what we want in life.

In this way, the past sets the stage for purpose. It has prepared us for the future.

From the past, we developed skills and abilities that we can use to implement our purpose.

From the past, we developed values and interests that point us to what is meaningful and satisfying.

From the past, we have created the circumstances and situations of our life into which we will express ourselves in purpose.

What's past is *prologue*.

As such, it's valuable to explore our pasts as it regards our pursuit of purpose. Knowing our authentic self and how it was formed points us forward in meaningful ways.

This week, you will examine how your past is relevant to your current purpose.

Shay's story illustrates how the past shapes our current purpose.

PAIN IN THE PAST PRODUCES A BEAUTIFUL FUTURE

Shay Walters is living a wonderful life. She's happily married with three children. She finds her work meaningful and enjoyable, and she's good at it. She's happy.

How did she get this life? Through lots of pain in her past.

Shay started drinking in high school. Then it was marijuana, pills, hallucinogens, and heroin. She was unafraid to try anything, and she got hooked.

Drug addiction became Shay's life. She lived just for the next fix. Eventually, she lost all hope of ever recovering. She just assumed that she would die an addict—probably sooner rather than later. She attempted suicide multiple times.

Her addiction devastated other people's lives as well.

Shay had her son when she was seventeen. When he was one year old, she overdosed with him next to her in bed. When he was two, he visited her in prison—beating against the glass, screaming, and crying. At three, he saw her get her head split open with a brick. At four, he was in a car accident with her as she drove under the influence. At five, he was being raised by his grandmother. At six, the court removed his mother as his legal custodian.

Shay was in and out of jail for years. She was a nine-time convicted felon for DUI, assault, trafficking, and tampering with evidence. She was facing 22 years in prison. Unexpectedly, the judge had mercy on her and sentenced her to only four years.

In prison, she detoxed. Then, a member of a 12-step community visited her and shared the 12-step program with her. Shay was so broken that she would try anything. The program gave her the guidance, support, and spiritual connection that she needed to overcome her addiction.

After recovery, while still in prison, Shay resolved to live as good a life as possible. She decided to do the next right thing in every situation. She didn't litter. She didn't cut in line. She called her mother when she was supposed to. She sent gifts to her son.

Shay wanted to do more in the world than just rot away. Her life had changed so much once she detoxed that she wanted to help others make the same change. She knew that if she could do it, anyone could.

Eventually, Shay was released from prison. She volunteered to help addicts still in the legal system. Over time the courts gave her additional opportunities to work with addicts in legal trouble.

Now, Shay and her husband run a behavioral health center for addicts. Her work is needed and appreciated. Shay has developed a strong online presence. In this way, she connects with and helps many people. Featured on her Facebook page ("From Prison to Purpose") is a picture of her holding her teenage son, and both are smiling happily. She's come a long way.

While Shay knows the pain and destruction of her past, she's grateful for how it has prepared her for the life that she's living now.

"
We begin to find and become ourselves when we notice how we are already found, already truly, entirely, wildly, messily, marvelously who we were born to be. Anne Lamott
"

What are some of the important lessons of life that I've learned so far?

_____

_____

_____

_____

What small thing can I do this day to live more purposefully?

_____

_____

_____

_____

Did I experience purpose in the past day? (Circle one)

-2   -1   0   +1   +2

What's one thing I did that mattered to me? Why did it matter?

_____

_____

_____

_____

"

*Life can only be understood backwards; but it
must be lived forwards.* Soren Kierkegaard

"

What are some of the ways that my life so far has prepared
me to live out my purpose now?

_____

_____

_____

_____

What small thing can I do today to live more purposefully?

_____

_____

_____

_____

Did I experience purpose in the past day? (Circle one)

-2   -1   0   +1   +2

What's one thing I did that mattered to me? Why did it matter?

_____

_____

_____

_____

"

Take your inspiration and passion from your life story. Bill George

"

How have past challenges developed my skills and interests?

_____

_____

_____

_____

What small thing can I do this day to live more purposefully?

_____

_____

_____

_____

Did I experience purpose in the past day? (Circle one)

-2   -1   0   +1   +2

What's one thing I did that mattered to me? Why did it matter?

_____

_____

_____

_____

"

Don't waste your pain; use it to help others. Rick Warren

"

How has the past prepared me to serve others?

_____
_____
_____
_____

What small thing can I do today to live more purposefully?

_____
_____
_____
_____

Did I experience purpose in the past day? (Circle one)

-2   -1   0   +1   +2

What's one thing I did that mattered to me? Why did it matter?

_____
_____
_____
_____

"

If we will be quiet and ready enough, we shall find compensation in every disappointment. Henry David Thoreau

"

Which events in the past have shaped what I value?

_____

_____

_____

_____

What small thing can I do this day to live more purposefully?

_____

_____

_____

_____

Did I experience purpose in the past day? (Circle one)

-2   -1   0   +1   +2

What's one thing I did that mattered to me? Why did it matter?

_____

_____

_____

_____

"

The past is never dead. It's not even past. William Faulkner

"

Which of my past experiences are most meaningful to me?

_____

_____

_____

_____

What small thing can I do today to live more purposefully?

_____

_____

_____

_____

Did I experience purpose in the past day? (Circle one)

-2   -1   0   +1   +2

What's one thing I did that mattered to me? Why did it matter?

_____

_____

_____

_____

WEEK 6 REFLECTION

In what ways has my past prepared me to take the next steps in my life?

_____

_____

_____

_____

_____

Looking over what I wrote this week, what can I learn about purpose in my life?

_____

_____

_____

_____

_____

Based on what I've learned this week, what would it look like for me to
live with more purpose?

_____

_____

_____

_____

_____

_____

SHARE YOUR JOURNEY - STEP 2

HOST A PURPOSE PARTY

Here's a fun way to share your purpose journey with other people: Host a purpose party.

We get together with others for lots of reasons. Why not purpose?

This journal gives you lots of material that you can use for creating such a party. Sure, the cover says that it's a daily journal, but you can also think of it as a party planning kit.

It's simple to do. Schedule a time to get together with other people. Then, figure out which material from this journal you want to use to create an interesting, fun, and maybe even profound time together.

You could:

» Pick questions from the journal that you've found especially helpful. Then, as a group, take turns responding to these questions.

» Share something that you've learned about yourself from doing this journal. Then, have the others apply this lesson to their own lives.

» Read one of the stories in this journal and have the group discuss what they can learn from the story. People can also share related stories from their own lives.

This journal gives you plenty of material to share with others. Just add food and beverages, and you have a party.

Week #7

REMEMBERING REGRETS

Regrets are warning lights when it comes to purpose. They often happen when we've missed something purposeful in our lives.

Maybe we didn't do something that we really wanted to do. Maybe we did something that we shouldn't have done.

Regrets are surprisingly painful. They give us feelings of sadness and disappointment. They are holes in our experience created by something missing.

We naturally want to hide from our regrets, to ignore them. After all, who wants to feel bad? It's important to recognize, however, that regrets serve a valuable purpose. They can point us to greater purpose.

Regrets are teachers that identify what is important and what can be done in life.

Regrets are motivators. While our past can't be changed, our futures can. We want to make decisions to minimize future regrets.

Regrets give us a way to reinterpret what's possible in life that allows us to create more purposeful futures.

This week, you will explore how your past regrets can guide you now.

This story illustrates how regrets can fuel a search for purpose.

A LITANY OF REGRETS

By the time he was in his forties, Richard was consumed by regrets.

The outward circumstances of his life were good. He was happily married with wonderful children. His career was in a good place. But... there could have been so much more.

Growing up, his family had difficulties. Somewhere along the line, he started to believe that what he wanted didn't matter, so why bother acting on it? This became a theme in his life.

At school, teachers would tell his parents how much potential he had if he just applied himself, but he never did.

For college, he put little thought into where to go. He chose, by default, a college that was not too far away.

In college, he deeply wanted to spend a semester studying in India—a magical, beautiful place. It was possible, but he never applied for it.

After graduation, he had no idea what to do for work, so he just took a job recommended by a family member. It turns out that the family member, who did the job herself, disliked it, and so too did he.

Then he went into a career recommended by another family member. It was better, but it wasn't what he had really wanted.

He worked hard at his career. There was so much to do, and he wanted to be successful. As a result, he missed many sweet moments with his children. The family would go on trips without him. Even when he was with them, he was distracted by thinking about what else he had to do.

Eventually, his missed opportunities and wrong turns came to a head. He felt overwhelmed with despair. Mental health issues arose. He suffered, and he made other people suffer.

Being disengaged from what mattered most was too much to bear. He knew that he had to change. He set upon a journey to greater health and purpose.

He explored what would be most purposeful in his life. He read books, talked to people, and went on many, many long walks trying to figure things out. It took several years, but eventually, he became clear about the things that mattered most to him in his work, family, spirituality, and self.

Having discovered purpose in general terms, he wasn't sure how to live it out, so he started trying things. Most didn't work, but some did. The failure was frustrating, but it wasn't regret. He felt good about working hard to do what mattered. He wasn't just letting life drift by him. Over time, he's found things to do and ways of being that he finds fulfilling.

He still has moments of regret, but they are nowhere near what he had before. His regrets pushed him into a life of fewer regrets.

"

The greatest danger for most of us is not that our aim is too high and we miss it, but that it is too low and we reach it. Michelangelo

"

What is something that I am doing in my life now that I might regret later?

_____

_____

_____

_____

What small thing can I do this day to live more purposefully?

_____

_____

_____

_____

Did I experience purpose in the past day? (Circle one)

-2   -1   0   +1   +2

What's one thing I did that mattered to me? Why did it matter?

_____

_____

_____

_____

"

Twenty years from now you will be more disappointed by the things that you didn't do than by the ones you did do. H. Jackson Brown, Jr.

"

What is something that I am *not* doing in my life now that I might regret later?

_____

_____

_____

_____

What small thing can I do today to live more purposefully?

_____

_____

_____

_____

Did I experience purpose in the past day? (Circle one)

-2   -1   0   +1   +2

What's one thing I did that mattered to me? Why did it matter?

_____

_____

_____

_____

"

The bitterest tears shed over graves are for words left unsaid and deeds left undone. Harriet Beecher Stowe

"

If I were to die tomorrow, what would I regret most about my life so far?

_____
_____
_____
_____

What small thing can I do this day to live more purposefully?

_____
_____
_____
_____

Did I experience purpose in the past day? (Circle one)

-2   -1   0   +1   +2

What's one thing I did that mattered to me? Why did it matter?

_____
_____
_____
_____

"

It is never too late to be what you might have been. George Eliot

"

At the end of my life, what am I most likely to regret about how I have lived?

_____
_____
_____
_____

What small thing can I do today to live more purposefully?

_____
_____
_____
_____

Did I experience purpose in the past day? (Circle one)

-2   -1   0   +1   +2

What's one thing I did that mattered to me? Why did it matter?

_____
_____
_____
_____

"

Wishes are recollections coming from the future. Rainer Maria Rilke

"

What would it look like for me to live a life of few regrets?

_____

_____

_____

_____

What small thing can I do this day to live more purposefully?

_____

_____

_____

_____

Did I experience purpose in the past day? (Circle one)

-2   -1   0   +1   +2

What's one thing I did that mattered to me? Why did it matter?

_____

_____

_____

_____

"

The best time to plant a tree was 20 years ago. The second-best time is now. Chinese
Proverb

"

What's something that I regret not doing in the past that I could still do now?

_____

_____

_____

_____

What small thing can I do today to live more purposefully?

_____

_____

_____

_____

Did I experience purpose in the past day? (Circle one)

-2   -1   0   +1   +2

What's one thing I did that mattered to me? Why did it matter?

_____

_____

_____

_____

WEEK 7 REFLECTION

Which regrets from the past can I use to live more purposefully?

_____

_____

_____

_____

_____

Looking over what I wrote this week, what can I learn about purpose in my life?

_____

_____

_____

_____

_____

Based on what I've learned this week, what would it look like for me to
live with more purpose?

_____

_____

_____

_____

_____

_____

DESIRES IN LIFE

Life is full of little things that we just have to do. We have work tasks, to-do lists, demands from others, and so on. This is our reality.

Unfortunately, it's all too easy for these "shoulds" of life to block us from pursuing the true "wants" of life. When we focus only on the urgencies of the moment, we can neglect the most important aspects of our life.

Deep inside of us is buried our vision for what matters most in life. We experience this vision as desires. These are not simply whims or passing fancies. Rather, these desires are our hopes for greater purpose. They give us dreams to cherish. From these dreams, we make plans. These desires are the launch pad for meaning in our life.

Ideally, we both know our deepest desires and have put them into action. Unfortunately, all too often, we don't act upon them or, maybe worse, don't even know what they are.

In our quiet moments, we feel the absence of engaging these desires. We know that there's something more to life, but we're not sure what it is.

Plumbing the depths of our desires can be frightening. They challenge our status quo. They want to turn our lives upside down. What we truly want is often at war with how we're actually living our lives.

Still, it's only in engaging what matters most to us that we can live a truly fulfilling life.

This week, you will explore your desires for a purposeful life.

Burt's story demonstrates the power of acting on deep desires.

RETURNING TO UNFINISHED BUSINESS

Burt Fleischner was doing just fine managing a branch of a national bookstore. He was good at his job, and it paid him well.

But there was a problem.

Burt didn't like doing the work. The company's priority was sales, and for his branch to continually exceed the previous year's sales just wasn't a goal that moved him. While he did it, it left him unfulfilled. He got to the point where he didn't know how much more he had to give to the job.

Burt was in his early 50s. Many people in this type of situation would have just ridden it out until retirement and then looked for something more meaningful to do. Burt figured that this was how his life would play out.

One day a customer in the checkout line asked Burt a question that changed his life. She was buying books, and they started talking. She asked him what he would have wanted to do with his career if he hadn't gone into the book business.

This simple question opened Burt up to a profound realization: He still had time to do what he most wanted in life. He didn't have to ignore his deepest desires any longer.

The customer, it turned out, was a life coach, so he scheduled sessions with her. Together, they worked through what he really wanted to do, and it turned out to be a longstanding desire.

When Burt was a teenager, his older sister Alice went off to college. After a while, she started experiencing severe back pain. Tragically, she had multiple sclerosis. Her health deteriorated rapidly, and she passed away several years later. When Alice was sick, Burt spent a lot of time helping her. He would help her get around, do physical therapy, and eventually cope with being confined to a hospital bed.

Years later, when he was reevaluating his career, Burt realized that he had unfinished business. He wanted to help injured people get back to health. He wasn't able to save Alice, but maybe he could help others in their healing journey.

So, Burt became a rehabilitation aide at a hospital. He worked with physical and occupational therapists in rehabilitating patients with significant injuries and impediments.

Burt loves his job now. It is a step down in both pay and prestige, but it inspires and gratifies him. He's also very good at it. He has been nominated for employee-of-the-year awards multiple times. He likes his work so much that he even told his boss that since he started at the hospital, he's not "worked" a single day.

"

When you discover your mission, you will feel its demand. It will fill you with enthusiasm and a burning desire to get to work on it. W. Clement Stone

"

What's something in life that I feel compelled to do?

_____

_____

_____

_____

What small thing can I do this day to live more purposefully?

_____

_____

_____

_____

Did I experience purpose in the past day? (Circle one)

-2   -1   0   +1   +2

What's one thing I did that mattered to me? Why did it matter?

_____

_____

_____

_____

"
It isn't a calamity to die with dreams unfulfilled, but it is a calamity not to dream... It is not a disgrace not to reach the stars, but it is a disgrace to have no stars to reach for. Benjamin Mays
"

What's a big, wild dream that I have for the future?

_____

_____

_____

_____

What small thing can I do today to live more purposefully?

_____

_____

_____

_____

Did I experience purpose in the past day? (Circle one)

-2   -1   0   +1   +2

What's one thing I did that mattered to me? Why did it matter?

_____

_____

_____

_____

"

If you can't figure out your purpose, figure out your passion. For your passion will lead you right into your purpose. Bishop T.D. Jakes

"

What would I love to do—more than anything else—with my life?

What small thing can I do this day to live more purposefully?

Did I experience purpose in the past day? (Circle one)

-2   -1   0   +1   +2

What's one thing I did that mattered to me? Why did it matter?

"

Great minds have purposes, others have wishes. Washington Irving

"

What is something that my heart says that I should
be doing in my life, but I am ignoring it?

_____
_____
_____
_____

What small thing can I do today to live more purposefully?

_____
_____
_____
_____

Did I experience purpose in the past day? (Circle one)

-2   -1   0   +1   +2

What's one thing I did that mattered to me? Why did it matter?

_____
_____
_____
_____

"

On finding one pearl of great value, he went and sold all that he had and bought it. Matthew 13:46

"

What's something so important to me that I'd be willing to give up a lot to make it happen?

_____
_____
_____
_____

What small thing can I do this day to live more purposefully?

_____
_____
_____
_____

Did I experience purpose in the past day? (Circle one)

-2   -1   0   +1   +2

What's one thing I did that mattered to me? Why did it matter?

_____
_____
_____
_____

"

The purpose of life, after all, is to live it, to taste experience to the utmost, to reach out eagerly and without fear for newer and richer experience. Eleanor Roosevelt

"

What's something in my life that I am avoiding doing
because it feels "too big" or "too wonderful"?

_____

_____

_____

_____

What small thing can I do today to live more purposefully?

_____

_____

_____

_____

Did I experience purpose in the past day? (Circle one)

-2   -1   0   +1   +2

What's one thing I did that mattered to me? Why did it matter?

_____

_____

_____

_____

WEEK 8 REFLECTION

What changes in my life would I make if I acted upon what I truly desire in life?

_____

_____

_____

_____

_____

Looking over what I wrote this week, what can I learn about purpose in my life?

_____

_____

_____

_____

Based on what I've learned this week, what would it look like for me to live with more purpose?

_____

_____

_____

_____

_____

_____

SKILLS AND ABILITIES

Everyone is good at something. We have different skills and abilities—things that we just do better than other people.

Usually, we think of these skills and abilities in terms of getting things done or being recognized by other people. In addition, what we're good at can serve as signposts that point to our purpose in life. It's as if our skills and abilities want to be expressed in action.

It's as if we have been prepared to do something significant in the world. Not only have we been given the desire to do it, but we also have the ability.

In this way, discerning what we're good at doing gives us useful information for finding what's purposeful to us. We identify our skills and abilities and then think about how we want to apply them. Any skill or ability can be used in different ways. It might play a central role in what we do in life, or it might be connected in a less direct way. Either way, it's important to know what we're good at on our path to living more purposefully.

This week, you'll explore your abilities and how they connect to purpose.

Steven's story illustrates how following skills and abilities can lead to great purpose.

HIS SKILLS POINTED HIS WAY TO PURPOSE

Steven Lavine grew up in a small country town. His father was a doctor and his mother a pianist.

Growing up, he was consumed with the question of how to make a difference in the world. The answer, he knew, was in serving humanity, but he didn't know the best way for him to do it.

Steven loved literature. Reading put him into other people's lives. It showed him what people share in common. It connected him to other people. It highlighted the unhappiness that people experience.

Steven was skilled at literature. He could analyze and articulate its themes. He could explain it to others.

He went to Stanford and then Harvard to study English and American literature. After getting his Ph.D., he accepted a faculty position in the English department at the University of Michigan.

As a professor, Steven loved teaching. He was good at it too—receiving a major teaching award. He also discovered that he was good at administration. Academics are notorious for talking about change, meeting in committees, accomplishing nothing, and then feeling good about it. Steven was different. He got things done. Over time, he realized that he could use his administrative skills to make the world a better place.

Steven acted on his newly discovered skills and took a position as associate director for arts and humanities with the Rockefeller Foundation. This position combined his love of culture with his ability to manage.

Steven's work at Rockefeller was deeply meaningful to him. He gave talented people the opportunity to express their lives to the world. He knew that the right grant to the right person could make a career and add an important voice to society.

Steven continued to develop his administrative skills. He listened to people of diverse backgrounds and viewpoints. He strategically invested resources and managed other people.

Then something unexpected happened. He was offered the position of college president—at the prestigious California Institute of the Arts.

Steven thought it was just dumb luck. He felt completely unqualified and unprepared for the position, but he accepted it anyway. As he learned the job, he realized that his work as a professor and director had developed in him the skills necessary for being a college president.

Even as president, he continued to develop himself. Being a college president is a complex and difficult job. He did his best and learned from his mistakes. He faced a significant challenge after the 1994 Northridge earthquake that devastated the campus. Buildings were not safe to enter, and the cost of repairing the campus seemed prohibitive. The college might even have to close its doors. Steven worked intensely to plan repairs and to raise funds. Through his efforts, the California Institute of the Arts made a full recovery and became even better than before. Steven has had a biography written about him—*Failure is What It's All About: A Life Devoted to Leadership in the Arts.*

Steven served as president at the California Institute of the Arts for 29 years. This is a very long tenure for a college president. It happened because he went where his skills led him.

"
There is something that you can do better than anyone else in the whole world and for every unique talent and unique expression of that talent, there are also unique needs. Deepak Chopra
"

What are some of my unique abilities?

_____

_____

_____

_____

What small thing can I do this day to live more purposefully?

_____

_____

_____

_____

Did I experience purpose in the past day? (Circle one)

-2   -1   0   +1   +2

What's one thing I did that mattered to me? Why did it matter?

_____

_____

_____

_____

"

*The meaning of life is to find your gift. The purpose of
life is to give it away.* Pablo Picasso

"

What are some of the most important skills that I've developed?

_____

_____

_____

_____

What small thing can I do today to live more purposefully?

_____

_____

_____

_____

Did I experience purpose in the past day? (Circle one)

-2   -1   0   +1   +2

What's one thing I did that mattered to me? Why did it matter?

_____

_____

_____

_____

"

The person born with a talent they are meant to use will find their greatest happiness in using it. Johann Wolfgang von Goethe

"

What do people ask me for advice on how to do?

_____
_____
_____
_____

What small thing can I do this day to live more purposefully?

_____
_____
_____
_____

Did I experience purpose in the past day? (Circle one)

-2   -1   0   +1   +2

What's one thing I did that mattered to me? Why did it matter?

_____
_____
_____
_____

"

Ego loves prestige and glamor. When it comes to life purpose, your ego is the most significant enemy to overcome. Jayne Stevenson

"

What are things in my life that I'm not good at
doing that might interfere with my purpose?

_____

_____

_____

_____

What small thing can I do today to live more purposefully?

_____

_____

_____

_____

Did I experience purpose in the past day? (Circle one)

-2   -1   0   +1   +2

What's one thing I did that mattered to me? Why did it matter?

_____

_____

_____

_____

"
You are meant to work in ways that suit you, drawing on your natural talents and gifts.
This work, when you find it and commit to it - even if only as a hobby
- is the key to happiness. Dennis Kimbro
"

How can I spend more time doing what I'm good at?

_____

_____

_____

_____

What small thing can I do this day to live more purposefully?

_____

_____

_____

_____

Did I experience purpose in the past day? (Circle one)

-2   -1   0   +1   +2

What's one thing I did that mattered to me? Why did it matter?

_____

_____

_____

_____

Use those talents you have. You will make it.
You will give joy to the world. Bernard Meltzer

How can I spend less time doing things that I'm not good at?

_____
_____
_____
_____

What small thing can I do today to live more purposefully?

_____
_____
_____
_____

Did I experience purpose in the past day? (Circle one)

-2   -1   0   +1   +2

What's one thing I did that mattered to me? Why did it matter?

_____
_____
_____
_____

WEEK 9 REFLECTION

What are some ways that your skills and abilities can guide you in finding greater purpose?

_____
_____
_____
_____
_____
_____

Looking over what I wrote this week, what can I learn about purpose in my life?

_____
_____
_____
_____
_____

Based on what I've learned this week, what would it look like for me to live with more purpose?

_____
_____
_____
_____
_____
_____

PURPOSE AT WORK

Work takes so much time and energy in our lives that finding purpose in our careers is especially important.

Without purpose, a career can make us miserable, feeling as if we're wasting our time. With purpose, a career can be a source of energy and passion.

Multiple factors play into creating purposeful work. It engages our skills, interests, and opportunities. Often people have to make several attempts at finding the right work, and even then, it can evolve over time. When someone finds purposeful work, however, work becomes something much more than simply getting a paycheck.

How do we find purposeful work? The first step is to look for it. We try different jobs. We experiment with what's possible. We learn lessons about what is significant for us. All of this moves us into doing what matters most.

Purposeful work isn't just found. It can also be created. We can take an existing job and modify both how we think about it and how we do it to make it more significant. Researchers call this job crafting.

A good place to start your quest for purposeful work is knowing what you want in work. Being clear on your desires and values leads you to the type of work that is the best fit for you.

This week, you'll explore work that matters.

Berta's story illustrates the development of a purposeful career.

FINDING PURPOSE FOR HERSELF—AND OTHERS—IN THE C-SUITE

Berta Aldrich grew up in a small town in Iowa. She envisioned a good life for herself, but her options were limited. She remembered her mother instilling the notion that "success in life starts with a good education." So, she set her sights on going to college. When she told her father—who hadn't attended college himself—he informed her that she'd have to pay for it herself. She accepted it as a challenge. She went to the state university and worked two jobs to put herself through all four years of college.

Berta had always wanted a career in business. She enjoyed managing complexity, collaborating with others, and creating opportunities for them to succeed—the foundational skills of corporate leadership.

Upon entering the corporate world, Berta assumed that everyone believed these same truths. She thought they would be ethical and kind, like the people in her small town.

She was completely naïve.

As Berta climbed the corporate ladder, she encountered coworkers—especially senior employees—who, frankly, were bullies. They had gained some success themselves, and they protected it by pushing other people down.

She watched as these people went to great lengths to discredit others. They'd lie about others' character and use unethical tactics. They would sabotage projects and take credit for other people's successes. They frequently targeted women—especially high-performing women.

Berta experienced all too much of this bullying. Nonetheless, she kept focused on doing the right thing, driving great results, and helping others achieve their goals along the way. Over time, she worked her way into the C-suite of a multi-billion-dollar corporation. She treated the hardships that she experienced getting there as learning experiences. Throughout every situation, she studied the bully's tactics and figured out how to overcome them, using the information to help others as both a mentor and leader.

Berta wanted to ensure her daughter—who also wanted to go into business—did not experience the same hardships she and countless others had endured in their workplaces. Berta wanted to do something to make it easier for her daughter and other talented future business leaders.

So, she wrote a book, *Winning the Talent Shift*, on how to navigate the corporate workplace. It identifies the most pronounced barriers that people face from their coworkers and how to overcome them.

The book was discovered, published, and distributed across the globe. Due to its success, Berta now consults with corporations to identify and invest in the right leaders. She shows them how to identify and develop leaders who inspire others to greater performance (bertaaldrich.com).

Berta has always sought purpose in work. She doesn't do it for success, money, or status. Rather, she wants to do something bigger than herself and help other people succeed. This is her purpose.

"

Real success is finding your lifework in the work that you love. David McCullough

"

If all jobs paid the same, which job would I choose?

_____
_____
_____
_____

What small thing can I do this day to live more purposefully?

_____
_____
_____
_____

Did I experience purpose in the past day? (Circle one)

-2   -1   0   +1   +2

What's one thing I did that mattered to me? Why did it matter?

_____
_____
_____
_____

"

Far and away the best prize that life offers is the chance to work hard at work worth doing. Theodore Roosevelt

"

What's are some of the activities that I would most enjoy doing for work?

_____

_____

_____

_____

What small thing can I do today to live more purposefully?

_____

_____

_____

_____

Did I experience purpose in the past day? (Circle one)

-2   -1   0   +1   +2

What's one thing I did that mattered to me? Why did it matter?

_____

_____

_____

_____

"

The reward of our work is not what we get, but what we become. Paulo Coelho

"

If I had to change jobs for something completely different from
what I'm doing now, what would it be?

_____

_____

_____

_____

What small thing can I do this day to live more purposefully?

_____

_____

_____

_____

Did I experience purpose in the past day? (Circle one)

-2   -1   0   +1   +2

What's one thing I did that mattered to me? Why did it matter?

_____

_____

_____

_____

"

Make your work to be in keeping with your purpose. Leonardo da Vinci

"

How can I change my current work to make it more purposeful?

_____

_____

_____

_____

What small thing can I do today to live more purposefully?

_____

_____

_____

_____

Did I experience purpose in the past day? (Circle one)

-2   -1   0   +1   +2

What's one thing I did that mattered to me? Why did it matter?

_____

_____

_____

_____

"

Where your talents and the needs of the world cross, therein lies your vocation. Aristotle

"

How can I use my current work to make other people's lives better?

_____
_____
_____
_____

What small thing can I do this day to live more purposefully?

_____
_____
_____
_____

Did I experience purpose in the past day? (Circle one)

-2   -1   0   +1   +2

What's one thing I did that mattered to me? Why did it matter?

_____
_____
_____
_____

"

For, in the end, it is impossible to have a great life unless it is a meaningful life. And it is very difficult to have a meaningful life without meaningful work. James C. Collins

"

How much do I feel a sense of destiny with my work now?

What small thing can I do today to live more purposefully?

Did I experience purpose in the past day? (Circle one)

-2   -1   0   +1   +2

What's one thing I did that mattered to me? Why did it matter?

WEEK 10 REFLECTION

How much, if at all, do I consider purpose when making plans for my career?

_____

_____

_____

_____

_____

Looking over what I wrote this week, what can I learn about purpose in my life?

_____

_____

_____

_____

Based on what I've learned this week, what would it look like for me to live with more purpose?

_____

_____

_____

_____

_____

_____

HALFWAY-POINT REFLECTION

Congratulations. You finished ten weeks of this journal. Great work! The time and effort that you're investing in doing this journal are moving you forward into what matters most in your life.

At this point, take some time to reflect on what you've learned so far. Review what you've written and look for patterns and insights.

What have I learned about my life purpose?

_____

_____

_____

_____

_____

_____

_____

_____

_____

_____

_____

_____

_____

_____

_____

_____

_____

_____

_____

How do I want to live differently because of this?

_____
_____
_____
_____
_____
_____
_____
_____
_____
_____
_____
_____
_____
_____
_____
_____
_____
_____
_____
_____
_____
_____

Week #11

FOLLOWING INTUITION

In society, we hear a lot about the importance of rationality. The educational system teaches us how to think logically and analyze cause and effect. Rationality is held out as the best way to make intelligent decisions.

When it comes to finding purpose in life, though, rationality plays a role, but it's not the only way of discovering purpose.

For many people, intuition is just as important—if not more—in discerning purpose. Intuition is knowing something with a hunch or gut feeling. An idea or action just feels right to do, even if we don't know why.

Our intuitions can lead us in unexpected directions—ways that we hadn't considered before and it might not even make sense to us.

Learning to notice our intuitions is an art. We often experience them as small "inklings." Nonetheless, they can lead to the greatest moments of life.

All too often, we ignore our intuitions. However, living a purposeful life demands that we notice and act upon them.

This week explores your intuitions about purpose.

Pam's story illustrates how following intuition can lead to greater purpose.

DREAMING HER WAY INTO PURPOSE

Pam Muller was having trouble. She worked as an elementary school teacher for seven years, but she realized that it wasn't the right job for her. She and her husband wanted to start a family, but they were experiencing fertility problems. Her life felt chaotic, and she didn't know how to move forward.

At night, in her sleep, her dreams became increasingly intense. They were filled with tornados, tigers, and other powerful but seemingly random images.

Pam started to wonder if something inside of her was trying to send her a message. So, she started paying more attention to her dreams. Maybe they would give her insight into what to do. She brought a playful curiosity to thinking about her dreams. Even if she didn't know what they meant, she was open to them helping her.

She started studying how to interpret dreams by reading books and attending training. She learned that dreams represent the content of the subconscious mind. They express it with images and emotions—bypassing the logical part of the mind. They tap into a deep source of creativity.

Pam learned a four-step process for interpreting dreams. With it, images that before seemed crazy now made sense. They represented emotions, situations, and people in her life. She had a sense that her subconscious was trying to communicate with her. She started interpreting her dreams every morning when she woke up. As she acted upon what she was learning from her dreams, Pam started experiencing greater health, well-being, and happiness.

Her dreams even pointed her to a new career. She became a dream expert. She now helps people interpret their own dreams. In doing this work, she finds that through dreams, the subconscious leads people into greater purpose in life (sweetgeorgiapam. com). Intuitively, they are able to connect the dots of life in ways they never had before.

Pam's own work is deeply fulfilling as she helps people move forward into their deepest desires. Her life feels very purposeful, and it all started with exploring her intuition.

"

Follow your dreams, they know the way. Kobe Yamada

"

What do I daydream about happening in my life?

_____
_____
_____
_____

What small thing can I do today to live more purposefully?

_____
_____
_____
_____

Did I experience purpose in the past day? (Circle one)

-2   -1   0   +1   +2

What's one thing I did that mattered to me? Why did it matter?

_____
_____
_____
_____

"

Deep within each person, there is an intuitive knowledge of what she or he wants most in life. We only have to look for it. Joseph Campbell

"

How would I finish a sentence that starts: "Do you know what would be great...?"

_____

_____

_____

_____

What small thing can I do this day to live more purposefully?

_____

_____

_____

_____

Did I experience purpose in the past day? (Circle one)

-2   -1   0   +1   +2

What's one thing I did that mattered to me? Why did it matter?

_____

_____

_____

_____

"

There is no one who can give you wiser advice than you can give yourself: you will never make a slip, if you listen to your own heart. Marcus Tullius Cicero

"

In the past, when have I ignored a gut feeling and regretted it afterward?

_____

_____

_____

_____

What small thing can I do today to live more purposefully?

_____

_____

_____

_____

Did I experience purpose in the past day? (Circle one)

-2   -1   0   +1   +2

What's one thing I did that mattered to me? Why did it matter?

_____

_____

_____

_____

"
Farmer Hoggett knew that little ideas that tickled and nagged and refused to go away should never be ignored. For in them, lie the seeds of destiny. The Movie "Babe"
"

What gut feelings am I ignoring now?

_____

_____

_____

_____

What small thing can I do this day to live more purposefully?

_____

_____

_____

_____

Did I experience purpose in the past day? (Circle one)

-2   -1   0   +1   +2

What's one thing I did that mattered to me? Why did it matter?

_____

_____

_____

_____

"

Have the courage to follow your heart and intuition. They somehow already know what you truly want to become. Everything else is secondary. Steve Jobs

"

Which of my future plans get me excited when I tell other people?

What small thing can I do today to live more purposefully?

Did I experience purpose in the past day? (Circle one)

-2   -1   0   +1   +2

What's one thing I did that mattered to me? Why did it matter?

"

At times you have to leave the city of your comfort and go into the wilderness of your intuition. What you'll discover will be wonderful. What you'll discover is yourself. Alan Alda

"

What are some changes that my intuition might be leading me to make?

_____

_____

_____

_____

What small thing can I do this day to live more purposefully?

_____

_____

_____

_____

Did I experience purpose in the past day? (Circle one)

-2   -1   0   +1   +2

What's one thing I did that mattered to me? Why did it matter?

_____

_____

_____

_____

WEEK 11 REFLECTION

What gut feelings do I have about how I should live my life differently?

_____

_____

_____

_____

_____

_____

Looking over what I wrote this week, what can I learn about purpose in my life?

_____

_____

_____

_____

_____

_____

Based on what I've learned this week, what would it look like for me to
live with more purpose?

_____

_____

_____

_____

_____

_____

_____

WAVING A MAGIC WAND

When we make plans for the future, we have to balance what we want and what's possible. Sometimes we want things that we just can't have because we don't have the skills or the opportunities.

But, this creates a potential problem because it's easy to overestimate the difficulty of following a dream that we have for the future. All too easily, we think that our dreams are "impossible" rather than just "not easy." We end up not following our dreams because we think that they can't possibly happen.

Trying something new is usually difficult to begin with. However, with practice and experience, it often can become possible. We find new ways of doing it, ways that we didn't know before we tried. This is a common pattern in inspirational stories. Someone sets out to do something that initially seems impossible. Then, they figure it out.

This is why magic wand thinking can be valuable. Magic wand thinking has us look at what's possible in our lives, assuming that we have great ability and opportunity. Then we decide what we want to do. Basically, we focus on discerning what we really want without worrying—at least initially—about its difficulty.

Magic wand thinking opens our hearts and minds to desires that we may have ruled out as being infeasible. Being aware of these deep desires opens the door to truly magical living.

This week explores what you most want in life—even if it doesn't feel possible.

*Diane's story illustrates the power of pursuing
a dream even when it seems impossible.*

FINDING WHAT SHE REALLY WANTED TO DO

Diane Husson started her career doing public relations in the corporate world. She made good money, but she knew that it wasn't the right job for her. It did not stir her heart.

She started asking herself, "Why am I here?" Finally, she decided to go out and answer that question. She sold most of what she had and used the money to travel. She bought a one-way ticket to Europe and set off with a backpack on her shoulders.

In Europe, she visited churches and museums. The art that she saw moved her deeply. She felt an almost spiritual connection to it.

Eventually, Diane ran out of money and came back to the United States. But something inside of her had changed. She was not the same person who had left. She had learned that she wanted to make art. There was a beauty and creativity to art that she couldn't turn away from. She had to be an artist.

It was easy to dream about being an artist while looking at masterpieces. It was much more difficult to actually do it.

Diane first moved to San Francisco and started painting. Then she moved to Norfolk, VA, to be near family. While she loved being an artist, she wasn't sure that painting was the right form of art for her. Besides, the paintings that she sold weren't enough to pay the bills, so she was broke. So, Diane rebooted. She returned to the corporate world to make enough money to have another go at being an artist.

This time she tried ceramic sculpture. She put in long days with plenty of trips to art shows and craft fairs. Eventually, she had success. People were buying her work. Companies hired her to create art for their buildings. Even though she was successful at ceramics, it still didn't feel like the right art form for her.

Diane started exploring other mediums of art. She searched for several years—taking classes and talking with different artists. Eventually, she found what she was looking for.

Faux bois is French for "false wood." It uses concrete and steel to make sculptures that look like wood. It entails welding, sculpting, chemistry, and lots of creativity. Diane grew up in the forested area of Northern Michigan with long walks in the woods, so the natural look of faux bois appealed to her. She taught herself how to do it.

Diane specializes in faux bois-style garden furniture—benches, tables, and chairs. Each piece is unique. Her faux bois art sells for a good price, and it's in demand (fauxboisfurniture.com). She even has a waitlist! She receives offers to mass-produce her work, but she turns them down. That's not who she is.

When she started out as an artist, making a living at it seemed impossible. She tried anyway, not wanting to let go of her dream. While she eventually succeeded, it still was not easy. When she meets up-and-coming artists, they often ask Diane how to become successful. Diane warns them that the worst day in the corporate world is easier than the best day as an artist. She does this to let them know what they are getting into. Still, she loves her job. The beauty and joy that she's found with it make her very glad that she was not put off by the difficulty of trying it.

"

Don't wait for a genie to grant your wishes. That power is yours. Gina Greenlee

"

If a genie gave me three wishes for a more purposeful life, how would I use them?

_____

_____

_____

_____

What small thing can I do this day to live more purposefully?

_____

_____

_____

_____

Did I experience purpose in the past day? (Circle one)

-2   -1   0   +1   +2

What's one thing I did that mattered to me? Why did it matter?

_____

_____

_____

_____

"

What goals would you be setting for yourself if you knew you could not fail? Robert Schuller

"

What would I do differently in my life if I knew that I could not fail at doing it?

_____

_____

_____

_____

What small thing can I do today to live more purposefully?

_____

_____

_____

_____

Did I experience purpose in the past day? (Circle one)

-2   -1   0   +1   +2

What's one thing I did that mattered to me? Why did it matter?

_____

_____

_____

_____

"

Success doesn't come to you. You go to it. Marva Collins

"

What would I do with my life if I didn't have to work for a living?

_____

_____

_____

_____

What small thing can I do this day to live more purposefully?

_____

_____

_____

_____

Did I experience purpose in the past day? (Circle one)

-2   -1   0   +1   +2

What's one thing I did that mattered to me? Why did it matter?

_____

_____

_____

_____

"

All of our potentials for good are unlimited. Colin Beavan

"

If I had unlimited resources for doing something new in my life, what would I do?

_____

_____

_____

_____

What small thing can I do today to live more purposefully?

_____

_____

_____

_____

Did I experience purpose in the past day? (Circle one)

-2   -1   0   +1   +2

What's one thing I did that mattered to me? Why did it matter?

_____

_____

_____

_____

"

Lost time is never found again. Benjamin Franklin

"

If I had an extra hour each day to make my life more purposeful, what would I do?

_____

_____

_____

_____

What small thing can I do this day to live more purposefully?

_____

_____

_____

_____

Did I experience purpose in the past day? (Circle one)

-2   -1   0   +1   +2

What's one thing I did that mattered to me? Why did it matter?

_____

_____

_____

_____

"

If in your mind it was possible to take a sabbatical from work to reassess your life, what would you do and where would you go? David Whyte

"

If I could take six months off just to discover what's most purposeful in my life, what would I do?

_____

_____

_____

_____

What small thing can I do today to live more purposefully?

_____

_____

_____

_____

Did I experience purpose in the past day? (Circle one)

-2   -1   0   +1   +2

What's one thing I did that mattered to me? Why did it matter?

_____

_____

_____

_____

WEEK 12 REFLECTION

How would I change my life if I thought it was possible to achieve my deepest dreams?

Looking over what I wrote this week, what can I learn about purpose in my life?

Based on what I've learned this week, what would it look like for me to live with more purpose?

Week #13

DREAMING BIG

Is it possible to fully live an ideal life? Probably not completely. Our lives sometimes require compromise and settling for less than we want because there are limited resources and opportunities. Sometimes, we have to put aside what we want for what we need. That's the way that life works sometimes.

Though life sometimes requires compromise, we want to be careful not to forget our dreams for an ideal life. If we let go of these dreams, we start choosing what's easiest and most expedient in a given situation. Over time, settling for less becomes our default approach to life rather than an occasional necessity.

It's surprisingly difficult to keep our ideal life in mind. Doing this requires us to be aware of what we want while knowing that we can't have it fully. The distance between what we want and what we can have creates anxiety. It's a form of dissonance. Ideally, this dissonance motivates us to work harder at living an ideal life. All too often, however, it leads us to give up what matters most.

We do best if we keep our ideal life in mind regardless of how much of it we think can be achieved. When we're aware of our dreams, they push us forward into decisions and actions that bring these dreams to fruition.

Keeping our ideal life in mind requires courage. We have to accept the disconnection between dreams and reality. Letting go of either one diminishes our life.

This week examines your dreams for an ideal life.

Bud's story illustrates how a seemingly unrealistic dream can become real.

A MAN, A BOAT, AND A PURPOSE

Bud Brown had lived a successful life. He had been a businessman, a pastor, and a consultant to pastors. He and his wife celebrated their fiftieth anniversary. They were healthy with children and grandchildren.

At that age, many people start winding down their lives—enjoying what they already have and preparing for the end. Not Bud. He knew that there was still more to do in life, but he wasn't sure what. His plans for the future were vague.

Bud took a class on finding purpose. In it, he did an exercise that had him describe his ideal life in three parts. Which activities did he most enjoy doing? Who would he like to work with? Who would he like to help?

For an activity, Bud loves sailing. He had grown up in Minnesota, where he frequented the many lakes and rivers. For who to work with, Bud wanted to work with his wife. At this stage of their lives, they just wanted to spend time together. To help others, Bud wanted to assist pastors with their ministries and marriages.

When Bud combined these three elements, a vision for the future hit him like a bolt of lightning. He wanted to start a sailing ministry. He and his wife could take couples in ministry on multiday sailing trips. They would sail the boat together, and Bud and his wife would train the couple in how to communicate and work together more effectively. This idea combined a cruise, marital counseling, and career training.

Bud told the idea to his wife, and she liked it. She, too, had been wanting something new. Just a few months later, they sold their house in Arizona, moved to the Texas coast, bought a boat, and now they live in a marina. They offer their services to various groups, and wonderful opportunities are appearing (sedonaleona.com).

"

And one perfect day can give clues for a more perfect life. Anne Morrow Lindbergh

"

What would an ideal day for me look like from start to finish?

_____

_____

_____

_____

What small thing can I do today to live more purposefully?

_____

_____

_____

_____

Did I experience purpose in the past day? (Circle one)

-2   -1   0   +1   +2

What's one thing I did that mattered to me? Why did it matter?

_____

_____

_____

_____

"

Where there is no vision, the people perish. Proverbs 29:18

"

What is the best possible thing that could happen in my life this coming year?

_____

_____

_____

_____

What small thing can I do this day to live more purposefully?

_____

_____

_____

_____

Did I experience purpose in the past day? (Circle one)

-2   -1   0   +1   +2

What's one thing I did that mattered to me? Why did it matter?

_____

_____

_____

_____

"
Your profession is what you're put here on earth to do, with such passion and such intensity that it becomes spiritual in calling. Vincent Van Gogh

"

If I had my ideal job, what would I do each day?

_____

_____

_____

_____

What small thing can I do today to live more purposefully?

_____

_____

_____

_____

Did I experience purpose in the past day? (Circle one)

-2   -1   0   +1   +2

What's one thing I did that mattered to me? Why did it matter?

_____

_____

_____

_____

"

Let us be grateful to people who make us happy, they are the charming gardeners who make our souls blossom. Marcel Proust

"

How would I describe my ideal friendship?

What small thing can I do this day to live more purposefully?

Did I experience purpose in the past day? (Circle one)

-2   -1   0   +1   +2

What's one thing I did that mattered to me? Why did it matter?

"

We travel not to escape life, but for life not to escape us. Robyn Yong

"

What would be an ideal one-month vacation?

_____
_____
_____
_____

What small thing can I do today to live more purposefully?

_____
_____
_____
_____

Did I experience purpose in the past day? (Circle one)

-2   -1   0   +1   +2

What's one thing I did that mattered to me? Why did it matter?

_____
_____
_____
_____

"

A home is more than just where you live; it reflects who you are. Ty Pennington

"

What would be my ideal living situation—house, community, location?

_____

_____

_____

_____

What small thing can I do this day to live more purposefully?

_____

_____

_____

_____

Did I experience purpose in the past day? (Circle one)

-2   -1   0   +1   +2

What's one thing I did that mattered to me? Why did it matter?

_____

_____

_____

_____

WEEK 13 REFLECTION

What can I do to live out more of my big dreams for life?

_____
_____
_____
_____
_____
_____

Looking over what I wrote this week, what can I learn about purpose in my life?

_____
_____
_____
_____
_____

Based on what I've learned this week, what would it look like for me to
live with more purpose?

_____
_____
_____
_____
_____
_____

SHARE YOUR JOURNEY AND HELP OTHERS – STEP 3

WRITE A PURPOSE POST ON SOCIAL MEDIA

Finding purpose is necessarily inwardly focused. You examine your life, discern what matters to you, and plan what you'll do with it. From all of this, you learn essential things about yourself and your purpose in your life.

Why not share what you've learned with others?

One way to do this is on your social media accounts. On social media, we usually post light content—moments from our days, jokes, memes, and so forth. You can also share insights from your journey into purpose.

You could:

» Post what you're learning about your own sense of purpose.

» Share lessons about purpose itself and how to find it.

» Present material directly from the journal. This includes specific questions or quotations that you have found meaningful. You have our permission to share bits and pieces of the journal online.

Sharing your purpose online lets other people know what's going on inside of us. It expresses who you are becoming. Also, your sharing might help other people think through their own purpose. It should also spark interesting conversations online.

When you share, use the hashtag #purposejournal. This will help you to connect with other people who are also using this journal for purpose.

LOOKING FOR CLUES

Finding purpose often means doing something new and different with our lives. Yet, when we think about it, we often realize that we've had clues along the way about what we really want.

These clues show up in many different places. Our sense of purpose can express itself in the hobbies that we've chosen, the books that we've read, the activities that we have wanted to learn more about, and so forth.

Once we recognize these clues, we can learn from them. They suggest ways of moving forward and things to try. Sometimes, what we'll find purposeful in our future is a new way of doing something that we've found purposeful in the past.

In this way, purpose leaves clues in our lives, and these clues point the way to a greater purpose.

This week, you'll explore your past activities for clues about your purpose.

Jon's story illustrates how purpose can be found in existing activities.

FINDING PURPOSE AFTER COMBAT

Jon Macaskill served his country for 24 years, 17 as a Navy SEAL. He was in Iraq, Afghanistan, and off the coast of Somalia. He experienced numerous small-unit, special operation missions in a wide variety of hostile environments. Needless to say, it was an extraordinarily hazardous duty.

Jon suffered trauma. He lost good friends on the battlefield. This led to stress and anxiety. He started having very dark thoughts about his life. He was looking down dark paths he knew he didn't want to go down.

He wanted help and went to counseling. The counselor recommended that Jon try mindfulness training. Jon was reluctant at first. It wasn't the kind of thing that he was normally interested in, but he did it anyway. He found that mindfulness meditation helped him considerably. It gave him stability, a feeling of being centered, and a sense of peace without the side effects of medications.

Jon became an avid practitioner of mindfulness. Before long, other men in his unit saw how it benefited him, and they wanted to learn more. So, Jon taught them how to do mindfulness themselves.

When he retired from the Navy, Jon didn't know what to do for the next stage of his life. He knew that he could make a lot of money in a career like real estate or investing. Deep inside, however, he knew that wasn't what he really wanted.

Jon wanted to help other people. He wanted to do something that gave other people more fulfilling lives, but he didn't know how.

As he thought about it, he realized that he was already doing something purposeful. He enjoyed teaching people how to practice mindfulness, and he knew that it helped them. Jon decided to take this activity, which had just been a small part of his life, and do a lot more of it.

Now, Jon is a full-time consultant (macaskillconsulting.com). He helps veterans handle the stress of their combat experiences. He shows organizations how to create more mindful environments for their employees. He even has a podcast on mindfulness entitled *Men Talking Mindfulness*.

When Jon was looking for purpose, he didn't need to find something new. He took something that he was already doing and reprioritized it.

"

Reading gives us someplace to go when we have to stay where we are. Mason Cooley

"

What do the books that I read tell me about my purpose?

_____
_____
_____
_____

What small thing can I do today to live more purposefully?

_____
_____
_____
_____

Did I experience purpose in the past day? (Circle one)

-2   -1   0   +1   +2

What's one thing I did that mattered to me? Why did it matter?

_____
_____
_____
_____

"
Free time was the most precious time, when you should be doing what you loved, or at least slowing down enough to remember what made your life worthwhile and happy. Amy Tan
"

What can I learn about my purpose from how I like to spend my free time?

_____

_____

_____

_____

What small thing can I do this day to live more purposefully?

_____

_____

_____

_____

Did I experience purpose in the past day? (Circle one)

-2　　-1　　0　　+1　　+2

What's one thing I did that mattered to me? Why did it matter?

_____

_____

_____

_____

"

You never lose a dream, it just incubates as a hobby. Larry Page

"

In what ways do my hobbies reflect what I find purposeful?

_____

_____

_____

_____

What small thing can I do today to live more purposefully?

_____

_____

_____

_____

Did I experience purpose in the past day? (Circle one)

-2   -1   0   +1   +2

What's one thing I did that mattered to me? Why did it matter?

_____

_____

_____

_____

"

The more that you learn, the more places you'll go. Dr. Seuss

"

What do I love learning about?

_____

_____

_____

_____

What small thing can I do this day to live more purposefully?

_____

_____

_____

_____

Did I experience purpose in the past day? (Circle one)

-2   -1   0   +1   +2

What's one thing I did that mattered to me? Why did it matter?

_____

_____

_____

_____

"

I search for meaningful conversation wherever I may travel. Without it, I believe we lose the ability to not only understand others, but more importantly, ourselves. Dhani Jones

"

What do I really enjoy talking about with other people?

_____

_____

_____

_____

What small thing can I do today to live more purposefully?

_____

_____

_____

_____

Did I experience purpose in the past day? (Circle one)

-2   -1   0   +1   +2

What's one thing I did that mattered to me? Why did it matter?

_____

_____

_____

_____

"

As far as we can discern, the sole purpose of human existence is to kindle a light in the darkness of mere being. Carl Jung

"

Which activities have I found purposeful in the past but have stopped doing?

_____
_____
_____
_____

What small thing can I do this day to live more purposefully?

_____
_____
_____
_____

Did I experience purpose in the past day? (Circle one)

-2   -1   0   +1   +2

What's one thing I did that mattered to me? Why did it matter?

_____
_____
_____
_____

WEEK 14 REFLECTION

What can I learn about my purpose for the future from activities that
I'm already interested in?

_____

_____

_____

_____

_____

_____

Looking over what I wrote this week, what can I learn about purpose in my life?

_____

_____

_____

_____

_____

_____

Based on what I've learned this week, what would it look like for me to
live with more purpose?

_____

_____

_____

_____

_____

_____

SEEING PURPOSE IN OTHERS

Have you heard the expression "seeing is believing"? When it comes to purpose, the better expression is "seeing is recognizing."

Often, finding life purpose is an exercise in looking *inward*. We explore what we're thinking and feeling, and we examine our deepest desires.

Sometimes, however, we do well to look *outwards* to other people. The world is full of people living rich, meaningful lives. They can serve as examples of what is purposeful and how it can be found.

We can see in others something that we want for ourselves. We look at what they are doing, and something stirs inside of us. Even if we can't define our own feelings of purpose, we can recognize it when we see it in others.

There's an additional benefit to seeing our purpose in others. It makes the purpose feel more possible. If they can do it, maybe we can too. This puts the purpose within reach.

This week, you'll look to the lives of other people to clarify your own sense of purpose.

DISCOVERING PURPOSE IN BOOKS

Glenn Stanton has just the right job for him.

He directs the research unit for an organization that advocates social policy issues. Basically, Glenn's job is to follow his curiosity. He learns new things, and he shares them through his writing and speaking. He's written nine books so far, and he gives talks around the world.

Glenn is fascinated by what it means to be human—especially as it relates to being in a family. He explores questions such as: How does being loved in a family make us who we are? What happens to people when they are not loved in a family? How do families impact society as a whole? These issues matter deeply to him.

How did Glenn get here? He first recognized this type of work in the lives of other people.

Growing up, Glenn was not the intellectual type. He struggled to get "C" grades in his classes, and he did that much just to keep his father off of his back. When it came to ideas and learning, he was unsure of himself and tried to avoid them.

At 20 years old, something important happened. Glenn read his first full book as an adult—*Black Like Me*. It's the story of a white journalist who darkened his skin and presented himself as black for six weeks in the Jim Crow South. The journalist described his experiences and compared them to his life as a white person. His story powerfully illustrated the deep, systematic racism in everyday life.

Something caught fire inside of Glenn when he read this book. It showed him someone who used learning and writing to make the world a better place. Glenn wondered if he could do the same.

Glenn started reading more books. Through them, he explored the lives of other people. He learned what they did and what they were thinking. In a sense, he lived their lives with them. With each book, he felt satisfaction knowing more than when he started. Glenn became a compulsive reader and learner.

At 28 years old, Glenn went to college. He hadn't attended college before because he didn't see a need for it. Now, he had a reason to go. After graduating, he went to graduate school to study philosophy and history. After that, he took jobs that used his thinking and research skills. Over the years, he advanced in his career to where he is now.

Glenn discovered his purpose by first seeing something in others that he didn't even know was in him.

"

Each person must live their life as a model for others. Rosa Parks

"

What do I notice about the people I know who are living deeply purposeful lives?

_____

_____

_____

_____

What small thing can I do this day to live more purposefully?

_____

_____

_____

_____

Did I experience purpose in the past day? (Circle one)

-2   -1   0   +1   +2

What's one thing I did that mattered to me? Why did it matter?

_____

_____

_____

_____

"

Don't live the same year 75 times and call it a life. Robin Sharma

"

What do I notice about people who are *not* living purposeful lives?

_____

_____

_____

_____

What small thing can I do today to live more purposefully?

_____

_____

_____

_____

Did I experience purpose in the past day? (Circle one)

-2   -1   0   +1   +2

What's one thing I did that mattered to me? Why did it matter?

_____

_____

_____

_____

"

To be what we are, and to become what we are capable of becoming, is the only end of life. Robert Louis Stevenson

"

Compared to other people I know, how purposeful is my life?

What small thing can I do this day to live more purposefully?

Did I experience purpose in the past day? (Circle one)

-2   -1   0   +1   +2

What's one thing I did that mattered to me? Why did it matter?

"

Choose a career you love and you will never have to go to work. Denis Waitley

"

Who would I most like to trade jobs with?

_____
_____
_____
_____

What small thing can I do today to live more purposefully?

_____
_____
_____
_____

Did I experience purpose in the past day? (Circle one)

-2   -1   0   +1   +2

What's one thing I did that mattered to me? Why did it matter?

_____
_____
_____
_____

"

Blessed is he who has learned to admire but not envy. William Arthur Ward

"

What is something that I admire in some of the people I know?

_____

_____

_____

_____

What small thing can I do this day to live more purposefully?

_____

_____

_____

_____

Did I experience purpose in the past day? (Circle one)

-2   -1   0   +1   +2

What's one thing I did that mattered to me? Why did it matter?

_____

_____

_____

_____

"

The human is indissolubly linked with imitation: a human being only becomes human at all by imitating other human beings. Theodor Adorno

"

How can I be more like someone who inspires me?

_____

_____

_____

_____

What small thing can I do today to live more purposefully?

_____

_____

_____

_____

Did I experience purpose in the past day? (Circle one)

-2   -1   0   +1   +2

What's one thing I did that mattered to me? Why did it matter?

_____

_____

_____

_____

WEEK 15 REFLECTION

What do I learn about my own sense of purpose by how I react to other people's lives?

Looking over what I wrote this week, what can I learn about purpose in my life?

Based on what I've learned this week, what would it look like for me to live with more purpose?

RELATIONSHIPS

When we think of purpose, our minds naturally go to our work and career. In addition, however, we can find purpose in every other area of our lives. One such area is our social relationships with friends, family, and even acquaintances.

Purposeful living is closely intertwined with relationships.

Other people help us find our purpose. They have insight into our lives and can identify what's important and overlooked. They can encourage and motivate us to pursue purpose. They can serve as role models for how to act purposefully.

Purpose connects us with other people. It can lead to more interactions with other people. This creates friendships and partnerships.

Finding purpose is self-focused in that we examine ourselves. It's also very social in that it is impacted by others and connected to others. This is yet another way that purpose makes for a good life.

This week, you'll examine the interplay between purpose and relationships in your life.

Robert's story illustrates the centrality of relationships in living purposefully.

BECOMING A CAREGIVER

Robert Pardi's life was going very well. He had a job in investment banking that he enjoyed, and it paid great. His wife, Desiree, was in medical school on her way to becoming a doctor.

Then, just as Robert accepted a dream job in Abu Dhabi, their world turned upside down. Robert's wife was diagnosed with Stage 3B breast cancer right before her 31st birthday.

Robert instinctively put aside climbing the ladder in his career, and he spent the next eleven years taking care of his wife. What made his caregiving journey rather unusual was a heartfelt request from his wife. As she was studying to be a doctor, she feared she would be a danger to herself by knowing the specifics of her situation. Therefore, it was Robert that retained all the critical information about her disease. He not only went to her appointments with her, but he was the one who spoke to the doctors about the state of her health. He helped her with whatever he could in whatever way possible. His purpose was simple—to be her caregiver and support her in living the life that she wanted. He came to define purpose like this: when passions fit with values, and one wants to give the results away to help another. It also became clear to him that caregiving was not about fixing but about supporting loved ones to live the best life possible while they were alive.

Robert's caregiving expanded. When he was at her appointments, he saw other people also undergoing cancer treatment by themselves—alone and unsupported. Robert became a chemotherapy companion for these other patients as well.

Then, after 11 years, Robert's wife died from cancer. He was grief-stricken and lost. He had no sense of direction. He numbed himself however possible. He contemplated taking his own life.

Slowly, a dream emerged from the rubble of his shattered inner world. Robert is of Italian heritage. His family immigrated from Italy several generations ago. He and his wife celebrated her last birthday in Rome. He wondered if maybe he should return to Italy to live. It felt like a positive step forward, so he did it. He arrived in Rome without a job, not knowing anyone, and was not able to speak the language.

Through several serendipitous events, Robert ended up living in the Italian town of Pacentro. It's a beautiful mountain town in central Italy with only 1,300 residents. It's where his ancestors had originally lived.

When he was his wife's caregiver, Robert learned valuable lessons about life. He learned to surrender to a larger purpose. He learned how to be vulnerable. He learned that he couldn't fix everything. He learned to be resilient amidst crushing difficulty. All of these lessons forever changed his perspective and values.

Robert knew that it was also time to let go of a career that no longer fit with what he wanted in life. Investment banking had been good to him, but he wanted something more meaningful. He wanted to directly help people live fuller, richer lives like he had found. He returned to school to be trained as a life coach. Now he coaches people around the world on how to live beautiful lives (robertpardi.com). He has also written two books. He speaks around the world about what he calls "Possibility in Action." He forms deep, supportive relationships with the people he coaches. Relationships give him purpose.

"

In our life there is a single color, as on an artist's palette, which provides the meaning of life and art. It is the color of love. Marc Chagall

"

How can I act more purposefully with my family?

_____

_____

_____

_____

What small thing can I do this day to live more purposefully?

_____

_____

_____

_____

Did I experience purpose in the past day? (Circle one)

-2   -1   0   +1   +2

What's one thing I did that mattered to me? Why did it matter?

_____

_____

_____

_____

"

Part of your purpose in life is to build strong and fruitful relationships with others. Zig Ziglar

"

How can I act more purposely with my friends?

_____
_____
_____
_____

What small thing can I do today to live more purposefully?

_____
_____
_____
_____

Did I experience purpose in the past day? (Circle one)

-2   -1   0   +1   +2

What's one thing I did that mattered to me? Why did it matter?

_____
_____
_____
_____

"

Let there be no purpose in friendship save the deepening of the spirit. Khalil Gibran

"

How can I act more purposely with my colleagues at work or school?

What small thing can I do this day to live more purposefully?

Did I experience purpose in the past day? (Circle one)

-2   -1   0   +1   +2

What's one thing I did that mattered to me? Why did it matter?

"

It is other life; it is love, which gives your life meaning. This is harmony. We must discover the joy of each other, the joy of challenge, the joy of growth. Mitsugi Saotome

"

How do people in my life encourage me to live more purposefully?

_____

_____

_____

_____

What small thing can I do today to live more purposefully?

_____

_____

_____

_____

Did I experience purpose in the past day? (Circle one)

-2   -1   0   +1   +2

What's one thing I did that mattered to me? Why did it matter?

_____

_____

_____

_____

"

Without doubt, the most common weakness of all human beings is the habit of leaving their minds open to the negative influence of other people. Napoleon Hill

"

How might other people actually hinder me from living purposefully?

_____

_____

_____

_____

What small thing can I do this day to live more purposefully?

_____

_____

_____

_____

Did I experience purpose in the past day? (Circle one)

-2   -1   0   +1   +2

What's one thing I did that mattered to me? Why did it matter?

_____

_____

_____

_____

"

Love is our true destiny. We do not find the meaning of life by ourselves alone - we find it with another. Thomas Merton

"

How might living purposefully improve my relationships with others?

_____
_____
_____
_____

What small thing can I do today to live more purposefully?

_____
_____
_____
_____

Did I experience purpose in the past day? (Circle one)

-2   -1   0   +1   +2

What's one thing I did that mattered to me? Why did it matter?

_____
_____
_____
_____

WEEK 16 REFLECTION

How purposeful am I in forming and maintaining my relationships?

Looking over what I wrote this week, what can I learn about purpose in my life?

Based on what I've learned this week, what would it look like for me to live with more purpose?

FACING DEATH

Purpose is all about life, and the best life possible is one with lots of purpose.

It's paradoxical, then, that facing death can foster greater life purpose.

Life is a limited resource. It will surely end someday, and the only question is whether that day will be measured in days, months, years, or decades. Death is one of the few certainties in life.

Being aware of our eventual death changes how we think about life. When we appreciate that our time is finite, we are motivated to use it more intentionally. There's only so much time available to make a life matter.

People experience this purpose-promoting aspect of death when they face life-threatening situations. These situations can be serious illnesses, bad accidents, or even the loss of a loved one. These brushes with death can bring forth a desire for purpose within us.

Even without near-death situations, we can harness the value of death for purpose by contemplating our own mortality.

This week, you'll use death as a way of clarifying your purpose.

Steve's story demonstrates how being aware of death can benefit life.

FALLING 100 FEET INTO GREATER LIFE PURPOSE

Steve Nelson was a hard-charging, type-A person. He ran 100-mile ultramarathons at an elite level. He enjoyed rock climbing and mountaineering. You could describe him as an adrenaline junkie.

One day, Steve invited a friend to go for a climb with him. His friend was going through a difficult time, and Steve thought that getting outside and exercising would cheer him up. They had climbed together many times before.

Steve took the lead, and he worked his way to 100 feet up a sheer cliff. Steve set up an anchor at the top for his partner to use and said he was ready to be lowered to the ground. Due to a miscommunication, Steve lost the anchor. Instead of being lowered, Steve fell 100 feet straight to the ground.

Somehow, Steve survived. Luckily, his injuries were limited to a badly broken femur and some broken ribs. Still, Steve was in bad shape. He required multiple surgeries to walk again, and his leg was now 3/8" shorter and rotated 9 degrees, so running was a challenge. After nearly a year, he was able to run again, but his days of competing at a high level were over.

When he fell, Steve thought he might die. When he survived, he had a different perspective on life. He wanted to live life more fully. He wanted to do more of what mattered most.

Steve focused more on his family—his wife, children, and grandchildren. He and his wife bought a home on a lake so that it could be a place for the family to enjoy their time together. The grandkids love visiting. Steve also started doing more things to help his family. He often helps his son-in-law and daughter fix up their house.

Steve still has lofty work and personal goals. That will never change. The near-death experience, however, made him realize that there's more to life than just accomplishing personal goals. He finds great purpose in the lives of those he loves.

"

Many people die with their music still in them. Too often it is because they are always getting ready to live. Before they know it time runs out. Oliver Wendell Holmes Sr.

"

How would I live differently if I knew that I had only five years left to live?

_____

_____

_____

_____

What small thing can I do today to live more purposefully?

_____

_____

_____

_____

Did I experience purpose in the past day? (Circle one)

-2   -1   0   +1   +2

What's one thing I did that mattered to me? Why did it matter?

_____

_____

_____

_____

"

What am I living for and what am I dying for are the same question. Margaret Atwood

"

How would I live differently if I knew that I had only one month left to live?

_____

_____

_____

_____

What small thing can I do this day to live more purposefully?

_____

_____

_____

_____

Did I experience purpose in the past day? (Circle one)

-2   -1   0   +1   +2

What's one thing I did that mattered to me? Why did it matter?

_____

_____

_____

_____

"

Live each day as if it were your last for some day it will be. Billy Graham

"

How would I finish this sentence: "More than anything, before I die I want to..."

_____

_____

_____

_____

What small thing can I do today to live more purposefully?

_____

_____

_____

_____

Did I experience purpose in the past day? (Circle one)

-2   -1   0   +1   +2

What's one thing I did that mattered to me? Why did it matter?

_____

_____

_____

_____

"

The best way to lengthen out our days is to walk steadily and with a purpose. Charles Dickens

"

If I live to age 90, how many weeks of life do I have left? (Subtract my current age from 90, multiple by 52). How does this number affect me?

_____

_____

_____

_____

How can I live out my values more fully in the coming day?

_____

_____

_____

_____

Did I experience purpose in the past day? (Circle one)

-2   -1   0   +1   +2

What's one thing I did that mattered to me? Why did it matter?

_____

_____

_____

_____

"

Death may be the greatest of all human blessings. Socrates

"

How does reflecting upon my eventual death make me feel?

_____

_____

_____

_____

What small thing can I do today to live more purposefully?

_____

_____

_____

_____

Did I experience purpose in the past day? (Circle one)

-2   -1   0   +1   +2

What's one thing I did that mattered to me? Why did it matter?

_____

_____

_____

_____

"

The purpose of our lives is to add value to the people of this generation and those that follow. R. Buckminster Fuller

"

What do I want my legacy to be for future generations?

_____
_____
_____
_____

What small thing can I do this day to live more purposefully?

_____
_____
_____
_____

Did I experience purpose in the past day? (Circle one)

-2   -1   0   +1   +2

What's one thing I did that mattered to me? Why did it matter?

_____
_____
_____
_____

WEEK 17 REFLECTION

How does reflecting on my eventual death make me
want to live my life differently?

_____
_____
_____
_____
_____
_____

Looking over what I wrote this week, what can I learn about purpose in my life?

_____
_____
_____
_____
_____

Based on what I've learned this week, what would it look like for me to
live with more purpose?

_____
_____
_____
_____
_____
_____
_____

MAKING AN IMPACT

Much of the work in our finding purpose is internal and introspective. We think about who we are, what we want, and what we're feeling. We follow our intuitions in moving forward.

The prominent internal aspect of seeking purpose doesn't mean that it's a selfish activity, however. Far from it.

Our doing the work to live purposeful lives invariably makes other people's lives better. This happens in multiple ways.

Purpose invariably connects us with other people. It's not a solo activity; rather, it leads us into other people's lives out of love. This creates loving relationships and community.

Purpose often leads us to directly help others. Altruism is a rich source of purpose in our lives. While there are many ways to be altruistic, they all give us meaning.

Purpose is inspirational. When we live the lives that we find most meaningful, we give others permission to do the same. We're modeling purposeful lives, and they can follow our lead.

Indeed, living purposefully might be the single most effective way of making the world a better place.

This week, you'll examine how your living purposefully can benefit others.

William's story shows how enacting purpose can benefit many other people.

I CAN'T DIE. I'VE GOT THINGS TO DO.

William McNeely wasn't feeling well, and he hadn't for a while. He never had enough energy. He didn't care about work. He even struggled simply coaching his son's football team.

Doctors tried various treatments, but the problem grew worse. William even started having trouble breathing. More testing found the problem. William had something called idiopathic cystic fibrosis. It is a terminal lung disease that progressively scars the lungs.

For the next several years, William took an oxygen tank with him wherever he went—work, errands, coaching. During one visit to the doctor's office, he saw that his chart was marked with the letters EOL. He asked the doctor about it. It meant "end of life."

As William contemplated his impending death, something stirred inside of him. He wanted to give back to his community of Charlotte, North Carolina. He wanted to leave a legacy that would go on after him.

So, William started planning. He envisioned a non-profit organization that helped children who had few opportunities or resources. William himself grew up in a single-parent family, so he knew what that was like. He was so consumed with making his plan happen that he told himself, "I can't die. I've got things to do."

Unfortunately, his body had different plans. Soon, his lungs started failing. The oxygen tank was no longer enough. The only possibility—and it was a longshot—was a double lung transplant. It wasn't even clear if transplant lungs would be available or, if they were, whether his body would accept them. But it was the only option that William had. He and his wife moved to the city where the transplant program was located. He started a preparation program for the transplant, but he couldn't complete it. His lungs were too far gone. The doctors gave him two weeks to live.

Then, a miracle happened. A pair of transplant lungs became available, and they seemed suitable for him. In a marathon surgery session, surgeons transplanted the lungs into William and waited to see what would happen. His body accepted the new organs. He still had to go through extensive rehabilitation, but he didn't care. He had his energy and functionality back. He didn't even need his oxygen tank anymore. He was alive!

With his new life, William founded the organization Do Greater Charlotte (DoGreater. org), a non-profit for children from under-resourced communities. It trains them in creativity, technology, and entrepreneurship. They learn job skills such as design, coding, and leadership. The children discover how much more is possible in their lives. They are inspired to pursue their passions, and they are given tools for doing so.

Do Greater Charlotte currently has a mobile lab that is driven to the children's neighborhoods. It's now building a much larger creativity lab in space donated by a local church.

William's brush with death crystallized his sense of purpose. This purpose, in turn, is transforming the lives of many people in his community.

"

You have a gift inside of you that only you possess. It was meant to benefit the world in some way. Delatorro McNeal II

"

If I could help any type or group of people in the world, who would it be?

_____

_____

_____

_____

What small thing can I do this day to live more purposefully?

_____

_____

_____

_____

Did I experience purpose in the past day? (Circle one)

-2   -1   0   +1   +2

What's one thing I did that mattered to me? Why did it matter?

_____

_____

_____

_____

"

Our prime purpose in this life is to help others. Dalai Lama

"

If I could help my friends and family in one way, what would I do?

_____

_____

_____

_____

What small thing can I do today to live more purposefully?

_____

_____

_____

_____

Did I experience purpose in the past day? (Circle one)

-2   -1   0   +1   +2

What's one thing I did that mattered to me? Why did it matter?

_____

_____

_____

_____

"

The way you get meaning into your life is to devote yourself to loving others, devote yourself to your community around you, and devote yourself to creating something that gives you purpose and meaning. Mitch Albom

"

How can I make my local community a better place for other people?

_____

_____

_____

_____

What small thing can I do this day to live more purposefully?

_____

_____

_____

_____

Did I experience purpose in the past day? (Circle one)

-2   -1   0   +1   +2

What's one thing I did that mattered to me? Why did it matter?

_____

_____

_____

_____

"

The sole meaning of life is to serve humanity. Leo Tolstoy

"

What problem in the world do I feel passionately about solving?

_____
_____
_____
_____

What small thing can I do today to live more purposefully?

_____
_____
_____
_____

Did I experience purpose in the past day? (Circle one)

-2   -1   0   +1   +2

What's one thing I did that mattered to me? Why did it matter?

_____
_____
_____
_____

"

The true meaning of life is to plant trees, under whose shade you do not expect to sit. Nelson Henderson

"

What could I do regularly that would make other people smile with joy?

_____

_____

_____

_____

What small thing can I do this day to live more purposefully?

_____

_____

_____

_____

Did I experience purpose in the past day? (Circle one)

-2   -1   0   +1   +2

What's one thing I did that mattered to me? Why did it matter?

_____

_____

_____

_____

" *By choosing your purpose in life—a purpose that serves the greater good—and devoting the majority of your time, energy, and attention everyday toward living it, you discover the secret to a life of fulfillment.* Hal Elrod "

How can I make someone's life a little bit better today?

_____

_____

_____

_____

What small thing can I do today to live more purposefully?

_____

_____

_____

_____

Did I experience purpose in the past day? (Circle one)

-2   -1   0   +1   +2

What's one thing I did that mattered to me? Why did it matter?

_____

_____

_____

_____

WEEK 18 REFLECTION

What are different ways that my own sense of purpose could benefit other people?

Looking over what I wrote this week, what can I learn about purpose in my life?

Based on what I've learned this week, what would it look like for me to
live with more purpose?

FINDING A CALLING

Do people have a calling in life? Researchers define a calling as feeling summoned to do something specific in your life. You can experience a calling from God, a higher power, nature, or just have a general sense that you're supposed to do a *specific something*.

A calling is recognized and received. It's not created by us out of our own interests. It's as if the purpose is already there. We just need to live it out.

When we experience a sense of calling with our purpose, it feels like we've been set aside to do something. It's a sense of destiny.

Having a calling changes how we live. It becomes central in our decision-making. With it, we rearrange our priorities, and we work hard to align our lives with our calling.

Not everyone experiences a specific sense of calling. All people with a calling experience it as purpose. However, not all people with purpose experience it as a calling. Nonetheless, it's worth exploring if you do have a calling.

This week, you'll explore the possibility of having a calling in your life.

Monica's story illustrates how a life calling is experienced and acted upon.

CALLED TO CARE

Monica Spooner and her husband already had five children when she was expecting Abby. When Abby was born, they found out that she had Down's Syndrome.

Down's Syndrome means different things to different people. For Monica and her family, Abby's birth brought richness and beauty. They learned deeper levels of love and sacrifice. They developed character. Caring for Abby brought them together as a family.

Monica had always enjoyed working with textiles. She found it meditative. She would often pray while weaving—reflecting on her life and what mattered most.

Not long after Abby's birth, Monica read a story in a textiles magazine about a program that taught disabled people how to weave fabric. Something stirred inside of Monica when she read it. She felt as if it might be a sign for the future.

As Abby grew up, she loved helping her mother weave. So, Monica taught Abby how to weave herself. The repetitious, mechanical nature of weaving was a good fit for Abby. She enjoyed doing it.

As Monica saw how much life weaving gave to Abby, she realized that she could use weaving to help other disabled people as well. So, she started a weaving workshop for them. This workshop now has a dozen weavers—all disabled (threadbendertextiles. org). They work together to make blankets, scarves, and other woven objects. This brings routine and value to their lives. They are proud of what they make and feel appreciated by customers who stop by the workshop and buy what they have made. The weavers feel connected to each other, and they have a shared sense of purpose.

Abby's birth brought many wonderful things into Monica's life—including a sense of calling.

"

Musicians must make music, artists must paint, poets must write if they are ultimately to be at peace with themselves. What humans can be, they must be. Abraham Maslow

"

What is something that I feel I was born to do?

_____
_____
_____
_____

What small thing can I do today to live more purposefully?

_____
_____
_____
_____

Did I experience purpose in the past day? (Circle one)

-2   -1   0   +1   +2

What's one thing I did that mattered to me? Why did it matter?

_____
_____
_____
_____

"

This is the true joy of life—the being used for a purpose recognized by yourself as a mighty one. George Bernard Shaw

"

What in my life has always felt really important to do?

_____

_____

_____

_____

What small thing can I do this day to live more purposefully?

_____

_____

_____

_____

Did I experience purpose in the past day? (Circle one)

-2   -1   0   +1   +2

What's one thing I did that mattered to me? Why did it matter?

_____

_____

_____

_____

"
*I believe each of us has a mission in life and that one cannot truly
be living their most fulfilled life until they recognize this mission and
dedicate their life to pursuing it.* Blake Mycoskie
"

What is something that I feel I am meant to do in my life now?

_____

_____

_____

_____

What small thing can I do today to live more purposefully?

_____

_____

_____

_____

Did I experience purpose in the past day? (Circle one)

-2   -1   0   +1   +2

What's one thing I did that mattered to me? Why did it matter?

_____

_____

_____

_____

"

Strange is our situation here on earth. Each of us comes for a short visit, not knowing why, yet sometimes seeming to divine a purpose. Albert Einstein

"

In what ways do I already feel that I am enacting a calling in my life?

_____

_____

_____

_____

What small thing can I do this day to live more purposefully?

_____

_____

_____

_____

Did I experience purpose in the past day? (Circle one)

-2   -1   0   +1   +2

What's one thing I did that mattered to me? Why did it matter?

_____

_____

_____

_____

"
Everyone has a purpose in life... a unique gift or special talent to give to others. Deepak Chopra
"

What talents and abilities have I been given to help other people?

_____

_____

_____

_____

What small thing can I do today to live more purposefully?

_____

_____

_____

_____

Did I experience purpose in the past day? (Circle one)

-2 -1 0 +1 +2

What's one thing I did that mattered to me? Why did it matter?

_____

_____

_____

_____

"

Seek a calling. Even if you don't know what that means, seek it. Phil Knight

"

What mission in life am I especially well-suited to do?

What small thing can I do this day to live more purposefully?

Did I experience purpose in the past day? (Circle one)

-2   -1   0   +1   +2

What's one thing I did that mattered to me? Why did it matter?

WEEK 19 REFLECTION

If I had to describe a calling in my life, what would it be?

_____

_____

_____

_____

_____

Looking over what I wrote this week, what can I learn about purpose in my life?

_____

_____

_____

_____

Based on what I've learned this week, what would it look like for me to live with more purpose?

_____

_____

_____

_____

_____

_____

BARRIERS ON THE ROAD TO PURPOSE

Once we identify what is purposeful to us, it's often difficult to move forward and do it. Enacting our purpose is an exercise in overcoming difficulties. One obstacle after another gets in our way to block our realization of purpose. It's almost as if something doesn't want us to do it.

Some of the obstacles that we face are external. We can have limited opportunities, existing obligations, or the disapproval of friends and family.

Other obstacles, however, are internal. We can feel afraid, which keeps us from changing. We can be distracted, which prevents change. We can lose confidence in what we're doing, which makes us want to stop doing it.

These obstacles are disheartening. We feel euphoria when we discover purpose, but then the difficulty of enacting it feels unfair.

In reality, the journey into purpose is one of struggle and overcoming difficulties. It starts with discerning purpose. From there, however, it's a fight to live it out. Somehow, the more significant something in our life is to us, the more difficult it becomes. Purpose is coupled with overcoming resistance.

Overcoming obstacles is valuable because it develops resourcefulness and resilience. These, in turn, make us better able to enact our purpose in the future. It's something of a paradox. The difficulties that we face when acting purposefully develop strengths that we need to live even more purposefully.

This week, you'll examine obstacles in your way of living purposefully.

All the purpose stories told in this journal feature someone overcoming significant obstacles that were blocking purposeful living.

ALL HAD OBSTACLES

Quan Huynh was serving a life sentence in prison.

Audrey Seymour was stuck in the wrong industry.

Nick Copenhaver hadn't taken the prerequisite courses for what he wanted to do.

Bob Turner was in the wrong career as a stockbroker.

Julie Cyzewski was in the wrong career as a special education teacher.

Shay Walters was a drug addict.

Richard felt crippled by regrets and lost opportunities.

Burt Fleischner was stuck in a job that he didn't care about anymore.

Steven Lavine felt completely unqualified for his new job.

Berta Aldrich was bullied at her workplace.

Pam Muller was adrift in both her personal life and her career.

Diane Husson was broke and didn't know which mode of art she wanted to pursue.

Bud Brown lived in the wrong place.

John Macaskill had combat-related PTSD.

Glenn Stanton hadn't read a full book before.

Robert Pardi's wife died tragically young.

Steve Nelson fell off a 100-foot cliff.

William McNeely was dying.

Monica Spooner had to care for a child with Down Syndrome.

"

He who has a why to live can bear almost any how. Friedrich Nietzsche

"

What is the biggest obstacle to my living more purposefully?

_____

_____

_____

_____

What small thing can I do today to live more purposefully?

_____

_____

_____

_____

Did I experience purpose in the past day? (Circle one)

-2   -1   0   +1   +2

What's one thing I did that mattered to me? Why did it matter?

_____

_____

_____

_____

"

It takes courage to grow up and become who you really are. e. e. cummings

"

What do I fear about living purposefully?

_____

_____

_____

_____

What small thing can I do this day to live more purposefully?

_____

_____

_____

_____

Did I experience purpose in the past day? (Circle one)

-2   -1   0   +1   +2

What's one thing I did that mattered to me? Why did it matter?

_____

_____

_____

_____

"

*Who you are, what you think, feel, and do, what you love
—is the sum of what you focus on.* Cal Newport

"

How am I distracted from focusing on what matters most in my life?

_____

_____

_____

_____

What small thing can I do today to live more purposefully?

_____

_____

_____

_____

Did I experience purpose in the past day? (Circle one)

-2   -1   0   +1   +2

What's one thing I did that mattered to me? Why did it matter?

_____

_____

_____

_____

"
Your mission starts where you are, not where you think you should be. Sometimes we're tempted to think that our current position/job/situation is a barrier to our mission, but, in fact, it is where it starts. John Ortberg
"

Which challenges must I overcome to live more purposefully?

_____

_____

_____

_____

What small thing can I do this day to live more purposefully?

_____

_____

_____

_____

Did I experience purpose in the past day? (Circle one)

-2   -1   0   +1   +2

What's one thing I did that mattered to me? Why did it matter?

_____

_____

_____

_____

> *The path to our destination is not always a straight one. We go down the wrong road, we get lost, we turn back. Maybe it doesn't matter which road we embark on. Maybe what matters is that we embark.* Barbara Hall

Which beliefs about myself hold me back?

_____

_____

_____

_____

What small thing can I do today to live more purposefully?

_____

_____

_____

_____

Did I experience purpose in the past day? (Circle one)

-2   -1   0   +1   +2

What's one thing I did that mattered to me? Why did it matter?

_____

_____

_____

_____

"

Go after what it is that creates meaning in your life and then trust yourself to handle the stress that follows. Kelly McGonigal

"

Why have I not committed myself even more fully to living purposefully?

_____

_____

_____

_____

What small thing can I do this day to live more purposefully?

_____

_____

_____

_____

Did I experience purpose in the past day? (Circle one)

-2   -1   0   +1   +2

What's one thing I did that mattered to me? Why did it matter?

_____

_____

_____

_____

WEEK 20 REFLECTION

How can I overcome the obstacles that I face in living a life of great purpose?

Looking over what I wrote this week, what can I learn about purpose in my life?

Based on what I've learned this week, what would it look like for me to live with more purpose?

Week #21

NEXT STEPS

How long will it take you to create a life full of purpose? It's more than a few days, weeks, months, or even years. Purpose is a lifelong pursuit. Yet, it always starts with a first step.

Your first step might be a small step. It might be a big step. Regardless of what you do, what matters is your movement forward into a life of what's truly important.

When you understand your purpose, seek opportunities to enact it. Become more effective in doing it. Learn about yourself along the way.

If you encounter a dead end, look for other ways to move forward. If it's taking longer than you expect, don't give up and continue pushing forward.

Ultimately, your goal is to fully devote yourself to moving into greater purpose.

This week, you'll explore the next steps in enacting your purpose.

The stories that you've read in this journal tell of people who faced significant obstacles but overcame them to live lives of great purpose. You can too!

ALL OVERCAME

Quan Huynh changed his thinking and behavior in prison to treat others with dignity and respect.

Audrey Seymour became a successful purpose coach.

Nick Copenhaver took extra classes during the semester as well as the summer session.

Bob Turner went into campus ministry and later moved his family to Africa.

Julie Cyzewski quit her job and went back to graduate school.

Shay Walters became sober one day at a time and now helps others as well.

Richard altered his career to pursue what mattered most to him.

Burt Fleischner quit his job to become a rehabilitation aide.

Steven Lavine became a college president.

Berta Aldrich made it to the C-suite and wrote a book to help others succeed as well.

Pam Muller became a dream expert to help other people.

Diane Husson tried multiple art forms until she found one that was just right for her.

Bud Brown and his wife sold their house, moved to the coast, and bought a boat.

John Macaskill learned mindfulness meditation and taught it to others.

Glenn Stanton started writing books and giving talks on his research.

Robert Pardi moved to a small town in Italy and coached other people into fuller lives.

Steve Nelson reoriented his life to family.

William McNeely launched a nonprofit organization.

Monica Spooner started a weaving center for adults with Down Syndrome.

What will your story be?

"
Figure out what your purpose is in life, what you really and truly want to do with your time and your life; then be willing to sacrifice everything and then some to achieve it. If you are not willing to make the sacrifice, then keep searching. Quintina Ragnacci
"

How can I become more focused on living purposefully?

_____

_____

_____

_____

What small thing can I do today to live more purposefully?

_____

_____

_____

_____

Did I experience purpose in the past day? (Circle one)

-2   -1   0   +1   +2

What's one thing I did that mattered to me? Why did it matter?

_____

_____

_____

_____

"
You can have anything you want – if you want it badly enough. You can be anything you want to be, do anything you set out to accomplish if you hold to that desire with singleness of purpose. Abraham Lincoln

"

Where in my life am I living most purposefully and why?

_____

_____

_____

_____

What small thing can I do this day to live more purposefully?

_____

_____

_____

_____

Did I experience purpose in the past day? (Circle one)

-2   -1   0   +1   +2

What's one thing I did that mattered to me? Why did it matter?

_____

_____

_____

_____

"

Efforts and courage are not enough without purpose and direction. John F. Kennedy

"

Where in my life am I living least purposefully and why?

_____

_____

_____

_____

What small thing can I do today to live more purposefully?

_____

_____

_____

_____

Did I experience purpose in the past day? (Circle one)

-2   -1   0   +1   +2

What's one thing I did that mattered to me? Why did it matter?

_____

_____

_____

_____

"
All successful people, men and women, are big dreamers. They imagine what their future could be, ideal in every respect, and then they work every day toward their distant vision, that goal or purpose. Brian Tracy
"

How can I change my daily routine to be more purposeful?

_____

_____

_____

_____

What small thing can I do this day to live more purposefully?

_____

_____

_____

_____

Did I experience purpose in the past day? (Circle one)

-2   -1   0   +1   +2

What's one thing I did that mattered to me? Why did it matter?

_____

_____

_____

_____

"

Each step you take reveals a new horizon. Dan Poynter

"

What are several big changes in my life that I might
consider making for greater purpose?

_____

_____

_____

_____

What small thing can I do today to live more purposefully?

_____

_____

_____

_____

Did I experience purpose in the past day? (Circle one)

-2   -1   0   +1   +2

What's one thing I did that mattered to me? Why did it matter?

_____

_____

_____

_____

"

What's the one thing you can do such that by doing it everything else is easier or unnecessary? Gary Keller

"

What is a change or two that I can make in my life that would substantially increase my sense of purpose in life?

_____

_____

_____

_____

How can I live out my values more fully in the coming day?

_____

_____

_____

_____

Did I experience purpose in the past day? (Circle one)

-2   -1   0   +1   +2

What's one thing I did that mattered to me? Why did it matter?

_____

_____

_____

_____

WEEK 21 REFLECTION

How can I overcome the obstacles facing me in my purpose journey?

_____

_____

_____

_____

_____

_____

Looking over what I wrote this week, what can I learn about purpose in my life?

_____

_____

_____

_____

_____

Based on what I've learned this week, what would it look like for me to live with more purpose?

_____

_____

_____

_____

_____

_____

LESSONS LEARNED

Congratulations! You made it. You've just spent 21 weeks exploring a deeper, richer life. You've examined your life from new perspectives to learn what matters most to you. Now, to crystalize what you've learned, summarize the key lessons that stood out to you. Identify the most important things that you have identified about your own purpose in life.

My Top Lessons

YOUR PURPOSE NOW

At the start of the journal, you described your purpose in life. Now, you'll do it again, having reflected on it for the last 21 weeks.

After you write this, compare it to what you wrote when you started and see what's changed.

How do I understand my life purpose now?

ACTION PLAN

In this journal, you've taken an in-depth exploration of your sense of purpose. Purpose, however, is more than just understanding. It's also action. Ahead of you, you have a life of putting into action what is most purposeful for you. To get you going, here is an Action Plan that you can fill out. It will help you crystalize the next right steps to take with your purpose.

PURPOSE GOAL 1

Describe the goal

_____

_____

_____

_____

_____

When will you start it?

_____

_____

_____

_____

Who can help you?

_____

_____

_____

_____

What is your desired outcome?

_____

_____

_____

_____

PURPOSE GOAL 2

Describe the goal

_____

_____

_____

_____

_____

When will you start it?

_____

_____

_____

_____

Who can help you?

_____

_____

_____

_____

What is your desired outcome?

_____

_____

_____

_____

PURPOSE GOAL 3

Describe the goal

_____

_____

_____

_____

_____

When will you start it?

_____

_____

_____

_____

Who can help you?

_____

_____

_____

_____

What is your desired outcome?

_____

_____

_____

_____

CONGRATULATIONS!

Stop. Reflect. Celebrate.

You've just completed a major milestone on your journey to discover your purpose. The last 21 weeks required energy, effort, and focus, and you should be proud of your accomplishment. We sure are.

We hope that you find yourself closer to discovering your purpose and are ready to take the next steps into truly embracing it.

Deep breaths. You got this.

We'd love to hear about your experience with this journal and where it's led you. Please feel free to email us at purposejournal1@gmail.com to tell us your story. Your story matters!

Congrats again,

Bradley & Andy

APPRECIATIONS

We greatly appreciate the many people who have given us their time and expertise to make this journal what it is. They include Susan Carozza, Giuliana Cipollone, Frank Cipollone, Elena Cipollone, Rachel Wright, Joshua Wright, Ed Cyzewski, Brian and Cindy Felkel, Lily Forand, Holly Johnson, Paige Long, Nidhi Nair, Irene Soteriou, Amina Jahanzeb Warood, Sam, Bob, Cory, and SJ.

We are especially grateful for the people who shared their purpose stories with us. Each one of them was a guest on the "School of Purpose" Podcast, which you can find on Apple, Spotify, and other podcast outlets. You can listen to their episodes to hear their full stories. You can find contact information for each of them in their episode's show notes.

Made in the USA
Middletown, DE
24 September 2024